About the A

CLAIRE NAHMAD lives in a tumbledown cottage in a remote part of Lincolnshire with her cockerel, Coleridge, and is the author of over twenty books on angelic and esoteric themes. She believes firmly in animal rights and recognises the soul forces of animals. Claire keeps a physic garden and believes that nature opens the door to consciousness of angels and the spiritual worlds beyond mundane experience. She is aware of sweeping but benign changes in education, science, medicine, social organization and human perception just around the corner, and feels that it would help to ring in these changes if society doesn't allow itself to disappear into cyberspace too much. It is her belief that we each have a secret contained within us, and that it is in the gradual revelation of this secret through the expression of our lives and our gifts that the world will be transformed.

KICK-ASS ANGELS

THE DYNAMIC APPROACH TO
WORKING WITH ANGELS
TO HELP IMPROVE YOUR LIFE

CLAIRE NAHMAD

WATKINS PUBLISHING

LONDON

This edition first published in the UK 2012 by
Watkins Publishing, Sixth Floor, Castle House,
75–76 Wells Street, London W1T 3QH

10 9 8 7 6 5 4 3 2 1

Designed and typeset by Mark Bracey
Printed and bound in China by Imago

British Library Cataloguing-in-Publication Data Available

ISBN: 978-1-78028-117-9

www.watkinspublishing.co.uk

Contents

This book is dedicated to
DONNA CUTHBERT,

in appreciation of all the sunbeams
she has sent my way.

Acknowledgements

Thanks are due to Mary Johanna, for her inspiring angel paintings and channellings. (*The Angel of the Rays* by Mary Johanna, Oughten House Publications, Livermore, California, 1997, can be purchased via the Internet.)

Many thanks also to Paul Kriwaczek, whose book, *In Search of Zarathustra – The First Prophet and the Ideas that changed the World*, published by Weidenfeld and Nicholson, London, in 2002, was an important source of inspiration.

Thank you to Dianne Pegler for her powerful mantra: I am Magdalene.

Introduction

A STRANGE PHENOMENON

Over a decade ago, an influence arising from Japan took root in Europe and rapidly evolved into a global phenomenon. It became known as reality TV.

Thereafter followed the numerous television shows that are popular today, involving individuals who are publicly tested, often in psychologically and even physically excruciating ways. They are then tried by a jury which includes the viewers. The process of elimination of participating individuals often incorporates ritual humiliation and castigation.

Why do these television shows attract such huge audiences? Why is there a universal appetite for them? And how are they connected with the angels?

Angelic wisdom seems to suggest that there is both a danger and a realization in our mass consumption of such material; a darkness and a light that pertain equally to a fast-approaching future for which we must prepare ourselves if we are to ride its transforming waves successfully and safely.

On the dark side, we appear collectively to be grasping desperately at old modes of thought: antiquated solutions to the challenges of life and society, which were discarded to some extent when the surge of idealism and humanitarianism that swept through western civilization after the end of the Second World War began to be converted into practical philosophy and social change.

The new thinking that asserted itself suggested harshness, authoritarianism, humiliation and chastisement were no longer the order of the day. They were regarded as the shadow of patriarchal Victorian values that must give way to modern enlightenment.

Yet, as the century progressed to its close and the ructions of extremism took their toll on America at the start of the millennium, as the crime rate soared, yob culture erupted wholesale and drug and alcohol addiction increased, many people began to rethink their stance on the old mentality. It seemed as if the crude, outmoded qualities of brutality and tyranny, rejected by our current western ideology but still very much in evidence on the global stage, might really be the way to get things done.

This latent admiration for what are truly unbalanced patriarchal values might be one of the significant reasons behind our enthusiastic planetary embrace of television programmes that degrade and humiliate their contestants. It is almost as if we enjoy spectatorship of these gladiatorial struggles because they bolster our return to a deep-rooted belief that the infliction of cruelty, discourtesy and degradation is somehow a good thing. They seem to confirm that life is, after all, an arena in which the symbolic wild beasts will claim most contenders as prey, and only the fittest can expect to survive. The vindication of such a philosophy satisfies our lower nature, which wishes to tyrannize, dominate, insult, chastise, justify the infliction of suffering, and to feel superior. Of course, the gladiatorial context is served up in a potent sugar cube of celebrity and money, which makes submission to the crude values of the old *modus operandi* even more alluring and compelling.

What do the angels, who are guiding us as a planetary community towards the challenges of our future, have to say about this strange phenomenon and the sway of the mentality it reveals? As far as I am able to interpret what they say, this is what I heard.

While some aspects of the mindset that it demonstrates are valuable, in that they represent paths of initiation which we all must walk on earth, and while we are certainly here on this planet to learn the lesson of deep humility (though never to purposely inflict it on others), there is grave danger in turning again to antiquated ways of thinking that served us in the past only at the cost of a war-torn world inhabited by oppressed individuals. For instance, in an episode of *The Apprentice*, Sir Alan Sugar said, 'I like her hunger for bull-dozing – she is ruthless, she will walk over anyone. That's what I like about her.'

Humanity has, for many thousands of years, been working toward a society that nurtures rather than cruci-fies. To throw our perceptual advances aside constitutes a real danger, a terrible danger, especially when we consider that there are forces abroad in our world, invisible but ever-present, which pro-actively wish us to take retrograde steps until we destroy ourselves and our planet via our own hands. They are no danger to us unless we permit them to be, but we have to be alert to them.

Yet, according to the angels, there is one thing that we are certainly divining accurately in our compulsion for such material – we need to pull ourselves out of a deep lassitude that seems to have descended on us just as we have reached the threshold of an entirely new era in human thinking and human being. The dawning day that waits beyond the door that we have opened will revolutionize every facet of our lives and deliver us into freedom. Yet still we hang back, uncertain and fearful, as if we want to believe that the great leap does not really have to be made.

Much ground has already been covered, of course. There is an ever-growing outcry against cruelty and injustice. Fields of new spiritual endeavour are opening up to us as never before. Quantum physics has confirmed that consciousness and reality seem to be one and the same. There is a shift taking place. Yet it seems to have stalled. We seem to have stalled.

When I was contemplating *Kick Ass Angels*, I was at first baffled by the task the angels had given me. I could feel the need for such a book, but at the same time I was unsure of how to go about writing it or even what its contents might be. I began to centre myself in the concept of the book, and, like opening a door onto a whirlwind, the Zoroastrian angels made themselves known to me!

The Zoroastrian angels are those revealed to the world by the ancient Persian mage, Zoroaster or Zarathustra. Zoroastrian priests were the famous Magi, known to commune with angels as part of their daily rituals. It was, indeed, Zarathustra who introduced to us the concept of angels as we understand them today. The orders of angels, particularly that of the archangels headed by Michael, are perceived in their traditional guise as a direct result of Zarathustra's illumination. In addition, his teachings on the God of Light and his adversary, the Lie, preceded the teachings of all the great religions, which echo them throughout their various doctrines.

The Zoroastrian angels wanted me to look again at a story of our human origins that I had intuited with

Margaret Bailey in a previous title, *The Secret of the Ages*.

In that book, we had traced what was to us the breathtaking and revelatory outline of momentous but hidden events in human history as they unfolded throughout the descent of the Abrahamic bloodline, whose origin was recorded in the ancient archives of the people of Sumer, many thousands of years ago.

Although, according to my perception of what the angels imparted to me, that story was confirmed as accurate, there was a vital element in it only touched upon in our work. That element was the huge significance of the biblical Ham (later termed Zarathustra) and his immense and heroic efforts to turn humankind away from the Shadow, or the Lie, which obscures the full wonder of our own humanity from us. Although we had indeed shone a light upon Ham in our book, his involvement with the story it told was so hands-on that it needed further revelation.

Throughout this book runs the story of Zarathustra (Ham), who, with his gift of revelation of the angels to humankind, prepared the way so that we could achieve an unprecedented spiritual breakthrough at this time in history. Zarathustra had a harrowing task to complete, as will be disclosed. He had knowledge of our beginnings as a human race, knowledge that has been forgotten today but is slowly being restored to us. He knew that his God of Light, and the obscuring Shadow or Lie that sought to divide us from that Light, had their human representations through whom cosmic and divine principles played.

Looking down the course of human history, Zarathustra saw that there were certain culmination points where humanity would be given a choice as to which road to take. These culmination points have been numerous, but a particularly vital one occurred towards the close of the nineteenth century.

It took place upon a mountain, as so many preceding it have taken place. It came to the philosopher Nietzsche, who represented humanity as it hung in the balance. Would he receive the impetus and enlightenment that would propel humanity forward, or would he misinterpret it and thus invite in the waiting forces of chaos?

From what transpired, and from the content of some of Nietzsche's great work, *Thus Spake Zarathustra*, we can surmise that the Lie left the imprint of its shadow upon the mind that was uniquely honed and geared to impel a significant community among the human family down a certain road. It should have been a very different road.

We stand at a similar crossroads today. The dividing of the way is already coming into focus. Will we cling on to old, selfish mindsets and unloving attitudes, as Nietzsche did, even while he seemed to be bringing in what was new and revolutionary, or will we at last take an evolutionary leap forward into freedom and our higher, greater selves?

Although we stand on the brink, overlooking the chasm, the angels assure us that we will successfully make the required leap – on the condition that we do not fall asleep again in the great Cloud of Unknowing that threatens to engulf us at the last moment.

What we need, it seems, are kick-ass angels! Kick-ass angels will ensure that we stay awake and, with a little prompting from behind, propel ourselves forward. The angels themselves are a little bemused by this choice of phrase, but they seem willing to stick with it for the time being, so that a point may be made humorously. Those entrusted with this task would prefer ultimately, I think, to be called awakeners or wake-up angels. They are essentially the Awakening Angels.

For now, I am sure they forgive my licence.

Chapter One
THE TIME OF THE KICK-ASS ANGELS

The kick-ass angels are coming! We have fallen asleep in a too-bland, fuzzy, wish-fulfilling dream of angels, and we need to wake up.

Kick-ass angels are not negative in any way; they desire only our progress and our awakening. They are not bullies or tyrants. Under no circumstances do they champion soul destruction, ungraciousness and contempt for sensitivity and finer feelings. They do not assume a critical or judgmental stance. They are not punitive, they do not chastise, they do not in any way use severity inappropriately – but they are kick-ass angels!

They are to do with releasing loving, positive free flow into negativity and devotedly nurtured old complexes. They are to do with cleansing, exorcism on many subtle levels, casting out fears and self-imposed limitations, changing stifling psychic air, identifying and challenging addictions and ingrained habits, and letting the winds of the spirit blow freely, like a bracing mountain breeze.

When we find ourselves suffering from subtle lethargy, stultification, blockages and stuck situations; when we seem unable to make progress and repeatedly encounter the same set of problems and circumstances; when our eye slips off the ball concerning our higher aspirations, we need to bring in the kick-ass angels.

When we feel our backs are against the wall, or that we are sinking in a steadily encroaching sea of inevitability, we can call on the kick-ass angels.

When we snuggle into self-complacency and our spiritual vision becomes shallow; when materialism and triviality threaten to hijack it, we can by prior arrangement give the kick-ass angels the go-ahead to intervene. When we feel resigned and hopeless, and the vital spark of our true self is dim and feebly flickering, it is time to summon the kick-ass angels.

Kick-ass angels are connected with our dragon essence. This sacred serpent essence is the magical flame of spirit that lies buried in our depths, in our soul. It is the sun within us. It breathes forth fire, and is a creature that lives and moves and has its being in the light. It is our purest, highest essence – the dragon essence within. It is our light body, our light being. It transforms us and our world.

It is connected to the kundalini energy that eastern adepts see as a coiled golden serpent dwelling in the chakra or power centre at the base of the spine. But it is not this sacred kundalini force we call on in order to connect to our dragon essence. Our higher and true dragon consciousness dwells as a flame in the heart. Summoning the kundalini serpent is dangerous and can lead to disastrous consequences. It can drive a soul mad, or apply the bellows of violence and aggression to its dimensions. The kundalini can all too easily feed itself into the belly of the lower dragon with its hideous rampaging strength arising from the forces of materialism. This lower dragon ever seeks to lock human beings in its coils and drag them off to its stinking lair. It is the dragon that St George, Archangel Michael, and other great guardians, are portrayed as 'slaying', or, more accurately, piercing through with spiritual consciousness so that it becomes transformed and offers up its imprisoned victims as well as releasing its own unique light.

After we become consummate with our true dragon consciousness, the kundalini looks after itself, and is stimulated naturally and safely.

When we call on the kick-ass angels, we call on our true dragon essence to arise and irradiate our consciousness. We become the Pendragon, literally the 'head dragon', which has three meanings.

The first is that our dragon essence has become our king or queen, our supreme ruler within. The second is that our dragon essence has risen from its throne in our heart to our head, to throw off supernal radiance from those two centres – the heart and the head – so that there is no misunderstanding or disconnection between them. They work and act in supreme harmony. The third is that the dragon of light within our deepest soul, in claiming its true inheritance as leader and inspirer and elected authority, has gloriously overcome the usurping dragon of the elemental forces. This is the lower saurian, the reptilian worm of wrath, who seeks to tyrannically oppress us and keep us in chains of enslavement in matter.

The kick-ass angels are those that foster, encourage and facilitate this process of overcoming the lower saurian. They are angels of the sacred light, of the golden serpent essence. They are the awakeners of the stars of measureless radiance that dwell deep within us.

Encountering these life-transforming angels of dynamic spiritual force allows us to locate our 'prison cells' and overturn the sentences we have, often unwittingly, imposed upon ourselves. They fathom our darkest, most fetid dungeons and unbind the aspects of us that dwell there, heavily manacled, in chains. They are unafraid of the gravest, unspoken, most horrifying secrets we may have buried in lonely places of denial and sad isolation.

The kick-ass angels are angels of resurrection, revolution and resolution. They are a burst of life everlasting. Their potency is in their wake-up call, for, as they themselves have intimated, the kick-ass angels are angels of awakening.

We need their help in our daily lives and our personal lives. We need their help to fulfil our potential. We need their help in realizing our spiritual selves. And we need their help collectively at this point in our history. Without the aid of the kick-ass angels, the transformation of the future cannot begin.

Chapter Two
WHO ARE THE KICK-ASS ANGELS?

The kick-ass angels are aspects of well-known angels, those we call on and who befriend us in every situation. They seem especially to be the great angels who guarded, enlightened, inspired and proclaimed to Zarathustra. They have always assisted humankind, and it is their nature to do so, kick-ass or otherwise! As we headed towards the nineties and left behind a decade devoted largely to materialism, there was a sudden explosion of interest in and communion with angels. This was a rich renewal indeed, and its benefits are inestimable. Yet, while it is wonderful that more and more people are persuaded to connect with the angels and ask for their help, it is true that there is also a danger of halting this transformation at the level of requesting protection and a parking space!

Even this degree of contact cannot be anything other than positive, of course, and as we open to angelic influence our lives are permeated on many subtle levels.

Nevertheless, the forces of the trite and the trivial are fighting back with a vengeance, and the angels themselves seem to be urging us to overcome them. It is important that our new-found angelic awareness does not deteriorate into a fashionable trend. It is important that we do not view the angels as a new way to get what we want on a superficial and self-absorbed level. Especially, it is important that the potential for transfiguration of our duller selves into the beings of light that we truly are and which will allow us to lay claim to our true humanity is not overlaid by the forces of worldliness, or what we might call the lower dragon, the dragon of the earthly mind.

This is where the kick-ass angels come in. It is their designated task to challenge these enervating, vampiric and disempowering influences. The kick-ass angels stand ready to transform sentimentality into a true heart-piercing by the sacred lance, to sweep aside banality and offer instead the light of a direct energetic transformation via our encounters with angels. They bring us the power of will to sacrifice indulgence of the lower mind in favour of a higher aspiration, and to become a receptacle for the spiritual and angelic consciousness that is our birthright.

Nevertheless, we can in truth think of the kick-ass angels as our own familiar and beloved angel friends. It is just that they want us to become much more keenly aware of their radiance, their reality, and their power to uplift us into realms of freedom and light.

A point worth reiterating about the kick-ass angels is that they are directly associated with dragon consciousness. Archangel Michael, for instance, who is certainly a kick-ass angel in one of his facets, is depicted as slaying the venomous lower dragon, but is also portrayed as a 'serpent of light'. He is spoken of in ancient texts as a 'pillar of flame'. The very early Chaldean scripture in which he first appears points to a link with Oannes or Enki, the god of light who was afterwards known as Ahura Mazda in ancient Persia and who, with his wife, taught the arts of civilization to the first human communities. It can be inferred from the texts that Michael stood beside Enki and his consort and was their great ally.

Enki channelled his teachings through the historical figure Zoroaster or Zarathustra. For those who love the angels, it is interesting to consider that what we know today of winged angel messengers who serve humanity with power and benevolence arose from the teachings of Zoroaster, particularly in Persia (modern-day Iran), for it was here that the Zoroastrian mysteries took deep root. Nevertheless, their origins can be traced back to Enki and therefore to the earliest culture of ancient Mesopotamia, from which the Persian civilization arose. Under Cyrus II, who was guided and inspired by these teachings, Persia became, in the sixth century BC, a global centre of excellence. Multi-cultural, multi-racial and multi-faith, it was known as the most enlightened nation on earth, where progressive and humanitarian values flourished and powerful inspiration in every field of human endeavour was crowned with fulfilment. Cyrus II was a committed Zoroastrian, and the sacred representation of Ahura Mazda, the Zoroastrian god of light, at the Persepolis in Persia is identified with the Sumerian Enki.

It is believed that there were many Zoroasters, as this was a titular name. A line of spiritual and genetic inheritance from Enki connected them. Their common ancestor was the biblical Ham who, it seems, from the consultation of sources more ancient than the Old Testament, was related to Noah but was not his son. (The Old Testament cites Shem, Ham, and Japhet as Noah's sons, but other, earlier sources quote Shem alone as the son of Noah.) A certain bloodline of a special nature (see below) connected Ham to Enki. Enki had fathered Cain, who was born to

Eve. It was this special bloodline that eventually produced Ham, the original Zoroaster.

According to the ancient Sumerian tablets, both Adam and Eve had come into being through a process of genetic engineering (a spiritual as well as a physical process). The sperm and ova of Enki and his wife (Nin-Khursag, Lady of the Mountain or Lady of the Tower, the 'great one') were utilized to convey the divine human essence into earthly animal bodies inherited from the simian line of evolution. This seems a fantastic notion, but in fact the Sumerian records attest to it in astonishing detail.

Ham gave forth the teachings of the true Father God, who loved and honoured Divine Mother, his source. These teachings eventually went underground because of persecution and wholesale denial, but they were kept alive by secret brotherhoods. The Zarathustrian teachings as we understand them today do not constitute the complete mysteries as they were once taught in remote times, although they certainly echo them.

Enki or Oannes (who became known as Johannes or John) remained as spiritual guardian of the secret temple whose teachings were finally given to humankind in full and perfect form through Jesus and Mary Magdalene. Their exposition of them was more advanced even than that of Oannes. He was a faithful and devoted son of God, and the enlightenment he and Nin-khursag provided for humanity was vital for its survival against the spiritual, psychic and physical odds that assailed it. Yet in Jesus and Mary Magdalene, the perfect son–daughter of Father–Mother God came into being on earth.

This couple was able to express in simple human terms the measureless glory of the Christ, the divine issue of the

ineffable Mother–Father, in all its dynamism and beneficence, in a pattern that could be understood and followed
by a confused and benighted humanity. Their ultimate gift
was the promise of the eventual baptism or 'christing' of
each individual so that they would be enabled to enter into
the essence of divinity and limitlessness, even while living in
a physical body on earth. It is this process and this promise
that the kick-ass angels seek to help us to embrace, and why
the angels whose essence is established and well-known
in our culture, such as Michael, Gabriel, Raphael, Uriel,
Haniel and Zadkiel, are numbered among them.

Chalchiuhtlicue

However, some of the kick-ass angels might be less familiar than others. Let us consider the angel Chalchiuhtlicue
(Chal-chi-uhtli-cu), for instance, who definitely belongs in
the kick-ass gallery.

The Mayans knew her well. They called her 'She of the
Jade Skirt'.

She is associated with the waters of the earth. Her
keynote is regenerative cleansing.

Think of her as a beautiful, swirling, washing energy,
imbued with the blues and luminous storm greys, the
foaming whites and the jade greens of the vast oceans. This
angelically coordinated forcefield is her 'Jade Skirt', with
which she accomplishes her formidable work.

Chalchiuhtlicue is the great exorcist of the kick-ass
throng. She casts out shadow forms and life-sucking entities that manifest as low moods, depression, chronic misery,
persistent ill health, pessimistic apprehension, self-doubt,
fear, anger and resentment. She delights in the restoration
of clear channels, free flow, unobstructed journeying.

Every sailor who has felt the lilt and lift of the waves and the high spirits they generate has found bracing attunement with Chalchiuhtlicue.

She is also an angel of birth and blessing. When we find the courage to embrace her impressive awakening potential, our bravery will be rewarded with gifts of recharging, realignment and new birthing in our lives, replete with the inevitable blessings they bring. Chalchiuhtlicue is mistress of the rapids, of torrents and whirlpools and tsunamis. She presides over the energy that can clear, cleanse and sweep away with full-on potential, but which can also devastate and drown.

She is the mighty force of inundation – the Great Inundator.

When we call on the kick-ass angels, we have to be very certain just whose ass we seek to kick! If it is our own, the veritable seat of all the heavy, wearying, unwanted energy and dark, life-draining consciousness we carry as a painful burden within ourselves, Chalchiuhtlicue will gladly be our saviour. We will be lifted, gasping and laughing, on the crest of her irresistible wave.

If we make the mistake of blaming others, including our various life situations, and summon Chalchiuhtlicue to sweep them away, the result will be horrifying indeed – for us! When we call upon her, 'She of the Jade Skirt' towers above us, speaking to us through the haunting, uplifting voice of the whales – the Cetacean nation – to which we can attune and connect through the inner, intuitive mind. She gifts us the invigorating power of her dynamism with a free heart and hand. But it is up to us whether we invoke the benign force, or the predation of the killer whale.

And if we are wise enough always to summon the former,

we may still expect to rise, somewhat shocked, on the spout which issues with such force from the Cetacean blow-hole! But Chalchiuhtlicue will be right there with us, teaching us to laugh out loud in our astonishment, counselling us to revel in the revivifying dance and interplay of the angelic forces that uphold us.

For our own safety and well-being, Chalchiuhtlicue teaches us not to blame, because in blame lies a drowning and swamping potential that lays us low. When we approach our problems and challenges without apportioning blame, the angels can speed to our aid down every route, including the kick-ass route!

In the intriguing, enigmatic Gospel of Mary Magdalene, lost to us for many centuries until it was rediscovered in an antiquities shop in Cairo by a German academic toward the close of the nineteenth century, Mary tells of an exhortation given by Christ: 'To be blameless is the true gift.' Christ preceded it by reminding his disciples that 'Love does not blame.' The context seems to suggest that blamelessness means not so much to be without fault, but literally to be blameless – to be without the habit or desire to lay blame.

The love of the angels beautifully resonates with this mystical teaching. When we apply it, we can be certain that our encounters with the kick-ass angels will be entirely positive and safe. Of course, the injunction includes refraining from self-blame. And if the tendency to lay blame does assert itself, the angels can heal it. Gently give your will into the safekeeping of the angels and ask them to bring you the gift of blamelessness. When you feel cleansed of the temptation to apportion blame, it will be safe for you to enter into the particular energy field of the kick-ass angels.

It might be said that the kick-ass angels are not for those who refuse to commit to the game of life, and yet, in another sense, when we are refusing to commit, they are exactly what we need. We only have to catch a fleeting glimpse of the 'other' will that stalks us to become alert to it and invite in the kick-ass angels. It moves stealthily between the trees of our intention, imagination and resolution, treacherously gathering in their solar power to itself and directing their force into pathways and destinations we do not want to follow and meet.

This is the will that overlays our own and, by an act of uninvited domination, overthrows it, leaving us feeling weak, helpless and humiliated.

This is the ruffianly will that ruins our best intentions and seeks to destroy our faith in ourselves and our progress. It is the force of self-sabotage. When it gains the upper hand in a human life, it says, 'No you can't,' every time a soul seeks to exceed its limitations or extend its horizons. It is this morbid anti-will that Chalchiuhtlicue washes clean until it is pure enough to reintegrate with the legitimate will of the soul, our real will that in such cases has become disempowered and superseded by a rogue, rebellious and reversed aspect of itself.

The vital point to remember is that we must not counter-mand our own will when bringing in the dynamism of the kick-ass angels. That would produce unhelpful and unpleasant results. It is unwise and unsafe to use the kick-ass angels in chastisement, as though we sought self-correction in a punitive way. Call on the kick-ass angels only when you are certain that your real will, the true intention in your heart, is in harmony with what you are asking them to do for you, and all will be well.

Over the next few chapters we will look at the leading lights among the kick-ass angels. Of course, these words must be taken lightly, because every angel is imbued with the special potential referred to as 'kick ass'. And, in case it might be forgotten how appropriately, gently and lovingly the angels apply this dynamic; in case a notion creeps in that it is somehow on a par with the mentality of popular TV programmes such as *The Apprentice* and *Dragon's Den*, it seems that the angels are counselling me to dispense with the 'kick ass' term! Instead, they suggest that I refer to them as the 'Ka' angels.

The Ka, in ancient Egyptian culture, was recognized as the soul. The lower astral body, which dismantles on death as does the physical body, was not designated as the Ka.

The Ka was the light body, that refined aspect of the soul which aspires toward a sacred marriage with the flame of spirit enshrined within the heart; the essential facet of the soul whose path is ascension and immortality. It is this vital and beautiful true self, the Ka, which the angels seek to reach and transfigure at the deepest level. And so we will advance from now on under the tutelage of the Ka angels, carrying with us the implicit understanding that they are indeed the kick-ass angels.

Chapter Three

ARCHANGEL MICHAEL, THE PENDRAGON

When working with the Ka angels, it is important initially to call on Archangel Michael, the Higher Dragon and chief of all angels, who is the great protector.

The dragon of everlasting light is actually *within* Michael. It coruscates as his glory, his source of radiance. It is a living symbol, a declaration that the lower dragon is eternally overcome. His consciousness radiates the might, the purity, and the greatest force of all, the consummate love that emanates in waves of light from the source, and is the source, which is God.

We can think of Archangel Michael as the supreme Pendragon, the deific originator of all the Pendragons who incarnated as earthly kings and queens. The Pendragon has a history that is worth examining, as it throws illumination on many areas of confusion. My own guidance has been that there is a flow of truth of the greatest magnitude in the story that can be pieced together from fragments of the ancient texts of Sumer, a civilization which arose in a strange and unprecedented flowering in Mesopotamia between at least eight and ten thousand years ago.

The first texts to mention Michael were from the Chaldeans, the last of the peoples of ancient Mesopotamia. Scholarship assesses their culture as one clearly arising from earlier Sumerian influences.

The Chaldeans worshipped Michael as a deity and a mighty guardian. His dragon inheritance can certainly be traced back to Sumer, because the earliest Sumerians, the Chaldeans' ancestors, understood God as the great Dragon Queen, 'She who bore them all'.

This was a monotheistic belief that dramatically predated that of Abraham and Moses, even that of their predecessor Zarathustra, and in fact is firmly linked to theirs. It was a balanced perception of the supreme deity in that it conceived of Mother and Father God as existing together in perfect harmony and equity, with the Father having been brought forth from the Mother as an aspect of, and an *a priori* presence within her. It was when the idea of an all-male God first took hold that the Dragon Queen, who had hitherto been worshipped as a wholly good and loving Mother God, began to be seen as the evil and degenerate purveyor of chaos and of all things bad.

According to ancient Sumerian texts, her sons (in the sense that we are all children of God), headed by Enlil the king and his presidential father Anu, were rulers of an advanced humanity overseeing the development of human life on earth. They initially introduced, as an aberration, the idea of male supremacy and of all things good proceeding exclusively from what was masculine and male dominated. They plotted against the Dragon Queen and 'slew' her, initiating humanity's long history of warfare, oppression and bloodshed. 'Slaying' her seems to mean that they purposely destroyed their direct and conscious connection with her. Humanity's link with God was obscured and difficult to comprehend from that point on.

The old texts that tell of these incidents seem to suggest that, as well as being God, the supreme generator of all creation, the Dragon Queen was also materially manifest in mother Earth, that the planet itself was of her and was her.

Her scheming sons caused a reversal of her divine forces, which attracted an extraterrestrial body to collide with her.

Afterwards, everything on earth changed. Enlil, pursuing his cherished ideal, attached himself as a guiding being of 'light' to Abraham (for the advanced humanity functioned on a higher vibrational wavelength than that of the simpler physical human beings walking the material earth), intent on influencing this great soul who would become the 'father of nations'.

Enlil had a brother, Enki, who held the right to kingship. However, Enlil had unlawfully seized it from him by force. Enki refused to become part of the conspiracy against Mother God. Instead, he and his consort initiated a secret temple that kept her knowledge and her mysteries alive. Enki was the great friend of earth's humanity. Enlil wanted to pursue a path that would lead it to destroy itself, and fought against Enki's operatives to civilize and educate it.

In the early days, the advanced humanity to which both Enlil and Enki belonged was known as the 'Serpent People'. The serpent in its true guise was recognized then. It was hailed as a symbol of healing and integration, of fertility and creation, of exalted love and mysticism, of the secret of life. Its progenitor, the Dragon Queen, manifested as such as an expression of the creative force that permeates the universe in exquisite, ever-giving, wave-esque expression. She gave the Serpent People some aspects of the serpentine form, which configured a beautiful humanity, as our simian inheritance does today.

Archangel Michael was one of the great archangels,

the mightiest of them all, who had come to earth with the Serpent People to initiate its humanity.

When humanity fell, egged on and undermined by Enlil, who was in himself the steepest gradient of its fall, the angels and the advanced humanity that remained faithful to the objectives of Enki and his consort could not remain. They ascended to a higher dimension and continued to help us from the spiritual realm. Enlil and his cronies were bound fast in an astral dimension from which, it appears, they continue to misinform and misdirect earthly humanity.

As the shadow of Enlil fell over the earth, the serpent became despised and reviled, associated with evil and particularly with women. What had once been the glorious symbol of the Sacred Feminine and its heart of wisdom now became the symbol of feminine foolishness, which began to be considered as the very essence of femininity. Enlil himself fostered this cultural and psychological process as an expression of his loathing of the Dragon Queen, Mother God, and as an obscene gesture towards the idea of a feminine god, especially the idea of the Divine Feminine as the original source of all.

Archangel Michael works with Enki and other great spiritual beings to redeem the earth from its blindness and ignorance. The consciousness of all these spiritual beings is conjoined and rooted in that ineffable force known as the Christ. Archangel Michael watches over the clandestine temple that Enki has striven to keep alive throughout the numerous centuries since Enlil's takeover – the Temple or the Church of John – which harbours the concealed, forbidden knowledge that will one day be restored to us.

Archangel Michael enshrines within himself the secret of the ages. The Shekinah – the essence and the radiance of God, recognized as feminine even by patriarchal mystics – shines forth from him in serpentine rays, the beautiful indwelling dragon of brightest brilliance, which is the star of the Queen of Heaven, 'she who bore them all'.

The dragon of light is within him, and is the jewel in his heart. Mother–Father God dwells in its deepest mystery, in harmonious balance and perfect equilibrium, telling this secret – that the Mother is the source, the origin, the ineffable one who bore Father God from her own heart and invested him with the divine potency of will.

For this reason, Archangel Michael is often referred to in the religious texts of antiquity as 'little Yhwh' or 'little God'. The name Michael itself means 'who is as God'. He is the angelic rendition of the unbroken circle of God.

Michael was given the particular care of a special bloodline that had been initiated on earth by ordinance of God. It bore a divine aspect. It replaced a wonderful power and light, a route of accessibility, which had hitherto been available to everyone on the planet until Enlil and his followers cut it off. We might think of it as humanity's direct link with God, which Enlil, perceiving her as the Dragon Queen, had despised and had striven with all his strength of black magic and power of reversal to destroy. The bloodline was not a perfect solution, but in our disordered world, it was the only one available. However temporary and imperfect, it had to remain in place until what Enlil had disempowered became reconnected. And the sole and only reason that it was put in place at all was that the gifts the bloodline bestowed on its inheritors might one day be given again to the whole of humanity.

As we are entering into Nazi territory when we speak of bloodlines, it is important to understand that, although the bloodline did give its offspring certain spiritual potential, it was always a matter of choice for any individual born of it as to whether or not they were able to avail themselves of its benefits.

It was essentially a facilitator so that highly advanced souls would be enabled to descend to earth via its accommodating DNA. However, this facilitation was still dependent on spiritual effort and right spiritual choice. The bloodline produced many spiritual 'duds' as it wove its way down the centuries.

It was of this bloodline that King Arthur was born. His was the greatest task that the world had seen – to establish Camelot as a global centre of spiritual excellence based on justice, compassion and divine inspiration, around which the human world would revolve until the point was reached where the breach that Enlil had inflicted could be healed, and humanity's direct link with God restored. He could not accomplish this monumental task alone, of course, and a mighty ally incarnated with him, an even greater soul than Arthur, who was destined to be his wife.

Sadly, Arthur rejected her in favour of Guinevere. The etymology of Guinevere's name shares an identity with 'ghostly' or 'shadowy' in the old Celtic language from which it derives. It has been pointed out by the author Callum Jensen that, in the spirit of the esoteric Language of the Birds (known also as the Green Language and the 'rabbit' language), said to reflect a universal mother tongue and whereby you 'say what you see', 'Guinevere' can be understood as 'Queen of Air', that is, as 'nothingness'.

Through the lens of my own intuition I seem to see, rather spookily, that Guinevere was *made,* like an incantation or an illusion, from which I can only deduce the possibility that, against her will, her own human essence was repressed and some other essence brought in to ensoul her via malignant rites. She herself was not evilly-intentioned, but she was the puppet of an intelligence that she allowed to manipulate her.

Nevertheless, King Arthur was and remains a great luminary, the ultimate earthly Pendragon. This titular name was given to him and to his line by the Druids, who prophesied his coming and oversaw his birth and childhood, wherein he was taught the mysteries of Archangel Michael, Pendragon supreme and spiritual ancestor of the bloodline, for Michael had fostered it since its inception. The vital symbol of the Druids was a golden serpent on a white background, denoting in one sense Archangel Michael, his colleague Enki and his consort, and their combined allegiance to the true God who manifested Her–His truth through the sacred serpent of wisdom.

It was Archangel Michael who protected Arthur and Camelot, building angelic essence into Arthur's great endeavour. When it failed, as it was bound to once Arthur had unwittingly turned his back on his true queen, Archangel Michael gathered up its essence and carefully preserved it in readiness to feed the vital spark of its dynamic into humanity's next huge venture to reconnect ourselves and our planet with God, which is happening today.

The spiritual teacher White Eagle tells us that Archangel Michael is the messenger from the centre of life, the first of the angels who head each of the Seven Great Rays of creation. A mighty spirit of the living Sun, wielding a bright sword of truth, he often manifests on a white horse, symbol of the purity and the spiritual verity of his message. He heralds the approaching dawn of the light of the spirit, which is destined to break worldwide, bringing the dazzling sunlight of the divine to every corner of our sad and burdened world.

Archangel Michael is a being of stupendous glory and transformative radiance, and it is his God-forged assignment, together with his feminine essence, the Shekinah, to direct all angelic beings as supreme leader and coordinator of angelic life in the heavenly realms, which interpenetrate and fecundate the earthly plane.

Human minds cannot conceive of any form of life existing on the Sun, yet it burgeons with intelligent life and consciousness. The Sun-spirits are embodied in a circle of light, like the Sun itself (human beings are based upon the figure of the pentagram).

The Sun-spirits have great rays of light projecting from their shoulders in the form of wings, with which they can propel themselves like flashes of light through the ether at unimaginable speed. There are countless spirits of the Sun, but the most majestic of the messengers who descend to the earth from the Sun is the one known to orthodox religions, and to faiths that predate these religions, as Archangel Michael. He is the ruler of all the life-forms on the Sun. He accompanies the Divine One, who has shone through Enki, Krishna, Christ the Messiah, the ideation of the Peace of Allah, Heah-Wah-Sah the ancient American First Nation leader, Amida Buddha, Brigid the White, and others, in varying degrees of brilliance according to their capacity, known by many other names throughout the ages of the earth. They are human renditions of the holy presence, which gives its life to all the suns of the cosmos and which stands above and beyond Michael and all the angels, and is known as the Divine Child of God, the son–daughter of the Mother–Father.

Unfailingly, when there is a new inundation of light, when the currents of divine love, wisdom and power are poured forth upon the earth, Archangel Michael encompasses the task, and is to be seen in his many guises by those with clear spiritual vision. When humankind can more readily receive and recognize his wisdom and love, we will duly be vouch-safed the revelation of the untainted wonder and beauty that we might create on the earth when the heart of every member of humanity is individually attuned and united with the heart of the universe, the heart of God, which is where Michael dwells and has his being.

The mighty sword of Michael is the sword of spiritual truth and enlightenment, which the Divine places in the hand of every one of Her–His followers – the incorruptible truth of the spirit, the pure spark of the Godhead alight within every human heart. White Eagle assures us that this is the weapon that guards us through every crisis of our human lives, giving us angelic strength to negotiate and overcome every impediment. When we invite Michael and his bright circle of angels into our lives, their power begins to manifest in our everyday experience.

The symbols of Archangel Michael are a sword of flame, the cross of light within the circle of light, and an ineffable trail of glory. He is Michael-Shekinah, the Sun-Radiant One. He is the strike of blue lightning that galvanizes creation.

In his Ka potential, he offers us this lightning strike. We may apply it to our lives and our aspirations, remembering always that it is the rod of initiation, the transformer of consciousness.

Chapter Four
KA ANGELS

Every angel has a Ka aspect, and there are many angels we
have yet to conceive of: angel companions, healers, bestowers and messengers who will help each individual setting
foot on the Ka path. Introduced below are a few of the
angels who might most readily be thought of as manifesting
Ka qualities.

(Var) Bahram

Var Bahram, Angel of Victory, stands glorious as a great Ka
angel. Michael and Shekinah are the initiating angels for
the Ka process, and the ones who will eventually bear us
up into victory. But they will carry us upward in company
with Var Bahram.

Var Bahram has always been associated with the ascent
of the human soul. He brings us a golden charge of dignity
and strength, which the darkness and its hypnotic elements
cannot resist. He can appear to the inner eye as a huge 'V'
of coruscating brilliance, throwing off gold flares like the
sun that ascends ever upward. When we see him like this he
is presenting his wings to our awareness and reminding us
that we can ascend above the lower things of earth via their
angelic power and vitality. We can embrace his angelic force
with our spiritual will and restore the potency of that will
when it has been undermined.

When calling on Var Bahram, we can also call on the Angel of the Sword to cut away from our psyche and emotional body any grasping tentacles or sticky adherence applied by aspects of our own pain and darkness. Just see this sword cleansing your soul and your soul-shrine or aura with vivid silver flashes, expertly and safely wielded by Archangel Michael, for Michael is the Angel of the Sword.

Balthiel

Balthiel is an angel who helps us to overcome jealousy and related feelings of inadequacy, bitterness and resentment. Enoch designated her as one of the seven grand planetary angels. She is also spoken of as 'the only angel who is able to overcome or thwart the machinations of the evil genius of jealousy.'

I have been given two images of Balthiel. One is as the presiding spirit of light over the abundance of a great harvest, as though like Ceres she overlights heavenly fields, wide as oceans, filled with swathes of radiant corn growing in abundance and, simultaneously, sheaves of corn waiting to be gathered into the granary. The other is as a bird of light rising high into the heavens above flames that cannot reach her, with a tail of living gold that drops angelic essence as gifts of healing and balm to the conflagration below.

Barbelo

Barbelo is known as 'a great Archon', next in light and magnificence only to God. Her name means 'perfect in glory'. As an Archon, she is a sovereign ruler among the angels who emits and fosters the communication routes between heaven and earth. She uplifts and inspires humanity to think in terms of spiritual vision and values.

She sheds a golden effulgence onto life's ups and downs, so that the breath and beneficence of Divine Spirit may be sensed through them, leading us home to the light of our eternal selves. She is the daughter of Pistis Sophia, procreator of the higher angels. The wisdom of Mary Magdalene is associated with Barbelo's divine emanation in the Gnostic gospels. Arcane lore designates Mary Magdalene as Pistis Sophia's voice on earth, and Barbelo as her 'sister'.

Aspirants of either gender can say, when calling on Barbelo or Pistis Sophia as Ka angels, 'I Am Magdalene'. See yourself enfolded completely in angelic wings, like a tower of light, and repeat the words as a mantra. This is a powerful invocation.

Chamuel

The beautiful angel Chamuel is one of the seven Archangels and chief over the order of Powers. Chamuel is the angel of Gethsemane, fortifying Jesus with the assurance of resurrection throughout the watches of the terrible night before the crucifixion. Chamuel is indeed a fortifying angel, bringing strength and resolution with which to face our worst agonies and apprehension.

Yet Chamuel is also an angel of gentleness, reminding us that gentleness is strength. Call on Chamuel to inspire tolerance and to soften harsh, critical, antagonistic attitudes. Chamuel helps us to love and to forgive ourselves, and to let go of a judgmental outlook on life, our own failings, and those of other people.

Charoum

Charoum is the Angel of Silence. When we need the dynamic of peace both within and without, we can summon the blessing of both Charoum and Valoel (*see* page 32). Charoum blesses the art of listening and teaches us to set a guard over our tongue.

He protects from inundation and, aligning himself to positive north, presides over this cardinal point. In the sound of his name is the rhythm of silence. If you create a measured chant from its repetition, softening the 'Ch' to 'Sh' and lingering on the second syllable, the soothing music of his name steals into the soul with a sense of profound hush.

The angels say that there is a mighty power in silence. It is the ineffable point from which all creation flows. Silence, in contradistinction to moroseness, empowers us.

The colour of silence is pure light, and those who can be graciously silent reveal themselves thereby as old initiates. They have mastered the art of silence, and they wear it as an auric crown of supernatural diamonds whose measureless purity is the essence of silence, for silence is the crown of enlightened consciousness. Let us remember the option of silence, with all its poise, dignity and peace. There is the deepest magic in it.

Colopatiron

Colopatiron is the angel who unlocks prison doors. Although he stands tall with great enfolding wings, Colopatiron can also appear as a moving point of light. He waits for you to hand him the key to your prison. You may not be able to operate the key yourself, but you must be prepared to yield it. Then, Colopatiron can joyfully fulfill his divine mission.

Consonia, Angel of the Violet Ray

Consonia is the angel of dreams and the bright half moon. She works from the violet ray of creation, which is the ray of the higher mind essence. In order to centre ourselves in our higher mind, we have to deal with our dark side. Buried trauma and heartbreak, broken dreams, fragmented hopes, self-hatred, soul-disfigurements, a record of the times we turned away from the light – all are hidden in our subconscious. It is like a well shaft that must be cleared in order to reach the purity of the starlit water below.

Consonia will show us how, and will be our guardian angel throughout this difficult but vitally necessary process. Consonia gives you her love and strength so that you may take a leap into the darkness, hand in hand with her angelic presence.

Elemiah

This angel blesses the depths of our self-awareness. He is one of the eight seraphim of the Tree of Life, associated with the dance of its continuous life flow. Call on this radiant one to illuminate blind spots, blinkeredness and ignorance, or distorted ideas of self. He is the angel of voyages, of maritime expeditions, of challenging soul journeys where we have to leave our comfort zones behind in order to expand our horizons and save ourselves from constriction and insularity. We must walk new lands and greet new dawns during these journeys. Elemiah helps us to do so in a spirit of adventure.

Gavreel

The Peace-Maker Angel, Gavreel resolves situations of enmity and conflict into forgiveness, acceptance and peace. As well as helping us to make peace with our enemies, Gavreel fosters mental and emotional balance and brings the balm of peace to troubled minds. Those enduring destructive stress or otherwise in need of equilibrium can invoke Gavreel and his merciful powers.

Although cited in masculine form, Gavreel is an aspect of Gabriel, whose manifestation to me seems deeply rooted in the Sacred Feminine. He is an emblem of her strength, and entered particularly into the perception of the Ethiopian Hebrews, who are rumoured to have the dangerously powerful Ark of the Covenant in their safekeeping. His special balm is that he 'keeps the invocant from going crazy in the night', which is a reassuring virtue for a Ka angel!

Haamiah

Haamiah is an angel of truth and integrity. To receive her kiss is to receive a brand of light that pierces every dimension of the soul. It causes no distress, but rather a wonderful release of confusion, a clearing away of unwise accumulation. When we withhold honesty from ourselves or others, it harms our soul. A mist covers our feelings and our relationships with others – a bewildering, distressing mist that makes everything, life's normal dynamics, seem stressful and traumatic. If you have lost sight of your own truth and you feel the resultant pull away from your centre, your integrity, call this angel into your field of spiritual vision with a sincere prayer for help. She will restore you to yourself.

Hahaiah (and Eleleth and Camaysar)

This beneficent one (pronounced Ha-hyer) ignites and fosters the beautiful flame of happy, positive and loving thoughts, feelings and impulses in our mind, heart and soul. She is the great angel set over ambassadors and diplomacy, and works with Gavreel to dispel regions of inner strife. As we will see, when we need the Ka angels to help us with situations wherein we feel that we are governed by two wills that conflict with or ignore one another, the angels to call on consist of Gavreel, Hahaiah, Eleleth and Camaysar. The angel Eleleth is a great luminary in Gnostic lore. The Gnostics said of him: 'the mighty Eleleth descends from before the Holy Spirit (the feminine essence of God); his aspect is like gold, his vesture like snow.' Eleleth has the power to reconcile the principles of ice and fire. Camaysar is an 'angel of the marriage of contraries'. He appears as a vision of light at the summit of a golden pyramid.

Jophiel

This great angel liberates our minds and our outlook from the bonds of programming and conditioning attached to sources that are not in harmony with the wisdom of our soul. He brings us emancipation, enlightenment, and the courage of open-mindedness. It was Jophiel who led Adam and Eve out of Eden so that they might become self-realized beings who could co-create with God. He offered Eve a bouquet of snowdrops as a sign of the returning cycle of hope and life in the depths of winter. His name means 'loveliness of God'.

Liromar, Angel of the Green Ray

Liromar is of the great sigh, heave and rhythm of the sea. She works from the green ray, the heart of things. She teaches us how to get in touch with our feelings, how to let the great charge of our emotions flow harmoniously throughout all the dimensions of our being. She returns us to the Nature of God, and to the cycles of nature, which are an expression of it. When you work with her, let Liromar be at your right-hand side, and her sister Consonia at your left. Yahriel also will shed her light over you as a benediction.

Maion

Maion is the Angel of Self-Discipline. She is associated with Saturn, the Tester. The Saturn angels are very benevolent and gracious to the soul that shoulders its tasks in good faith. They shine with a profound, austere brilliance and move with a slow majesty that seems to arise from great depths. This bright spirit holds up the ideal of wise self-regulation and denial of the demands and dominion of the lower self, but counsels against harshness. She reminds us that self-flagellation can be a form of indulgence! Attune yourself to this angel to learn the gentle but persistent art of self-governance.

Omniel

This angel fosters our connectedness with one another. He lifts us into Divine Oneness and heals our tendency toward isolation of self. Those suffering from loneliness, from autism, from imbalances in the ego, will benefit from the healing influences of this shining one. According to ancient texts, Omniel took great delight in 'mixing with mortals' prior to the Deluge. He was one of the benevolent, teaching angels who 'walked and talked with men' throughout the lost and lamented Golden Age.

Pyrhea, Angel of the Red Ray

Pyrhea governs initiating energy, grounding and the primal life force. This dynamic angel has tremendous Ka potency, but her power must be used wisely.

Rampel

An angelic guard set over great mountains, Rampel stands mighty, stable, steadfast and true. He belongs to the company of 'splendid, terrible and mighty angel chiefs' who passed before God to rejoice in Creation on its completion. Call on him for stability, strength and endurance, especially when something needs to be brought to resolution and fulfilment.

Shemael

Shemael fosters the upwelling of gratitude in the human heart. When these springs have run dry or become choked, depression and a feeling of disgust with life are the inevitable results. Energy does not replenish itself, and a person may put on weight in an attempt to draw mental and physical energy from food and the act of eating. When life seems grey, desolate and grief-stricken, it is difficult to feel gratitude for the experience of it.

Therefore, we treat depression and world-weariness with Shemael's gentle, compassionate gifts, so that the deep wellsprings of the spirit may be renewed. In Hebrew lore, Shemael is the mighty angel who stands at the windows of heaven, gathering in songs of praise to the Divine Spirit as they ascend like incense from the earth.

This clarifying symbol reveals the source of Shemael's name, which is derived from the first word of the Hebrew song of praise.

Tabris

This angel is set over free will, self-determination and independence of choice. We invoke Tabris when we need help to lift ourselves out of a stalemate or stuck situation and seek to become aware of creative alternatives. When thinking of Tabris, remember Colopatiron, the angel who comes to unlock the prison gate. Tabris and Colpatiron work together. They also grant mortals the necessary patience and endurance to wait quietly and alertly for that moment when the opportunity for their release comes.

Valoel

Valoel is the sublime Angel of Peace. We can call on this great one to bless us with a serene mind, a tranquil heart and with peaceful dreams. We can also ask Valoel to bring the balm of healing peace to an aggravated situation or relationship. Valoel works with Charoum, the Angel of Silence, and Gavreel, the Peace-Maker, to express her full potential. As a Ka angel, Valoel banishes disturbers of the peace. However, it is only the disruptive elements within ourselves that we should attempt to troubleshoot in this way. At the point where we are no longer prepared to continue to tolerate certain inner conditions, we can call on Valoel as a dynamic ally.

When we experience the descent of her presence, as a Ka angel or otherwise, we will understand the dynamo that is peace. It is related to the munificence of the creative power that informs silence.

The Virgin of Light

The Virgin of Light is a mighty angel of the Order of Virtues, dwelling in the moon.

We can contact all angels through the action of angel-attuned breathing, but the Virgin of Light particularly so. We can summon her almost instantly via our breath and inner vision. She comes alight within us like a great lamp of the heavens, infinitely bright with a silvery brilliance and a calm, still pulchritude. She lights the way when our intuition is benighted and stumbles. As a Ka angel, she sheds light on areas that we would rather keep darkened, and yet by doing so are disconnecting from inner wisdom.

The Virtues

We call on the Virtues when we need a transformation of conditions or circumstances. They are a high order of angels whose principal duty is to work miracles on earth. As Ka angels, they are bestowers of grace and valour.

Vohu Manah ('Good Thought')

This wonderful angel blesses and uplifts our thoughts and our thought-sphere (the vessel which generates, contains, attracts, reflects and distributes our thoughts). When suffering from a negative, anxious or pessimistic outlook, or harbouring angry, conceited or otherwise inharmonious thought-energy, we need to be brought before Vohu Manah.

This angel will be discussed at length in a separate chapter. The full impact of the Ka angels cannot be received without the attuning power of the positive vibrations of 'good thought'.

Vwyamus

The great cleansing angel Vwyamus (Vwy-ah-mus) has the power to clear our surroundings and our aura of negative vibrations and accumulated psychic material. Vwyamus has power over the unpleasant etheric mucus that gathers in our immediate environment and within our auric field. This etherically viscous substance has the same effect as physical mucus in that it blocks our spiritual breathing and hearing passages, poisons our system and generally makes us feel off-colour. The dynamic cleansing and clearing virtues of Vwyamus dissolve and purify all forms of etheric mucus, absorbing it into the heart of high-spinning angelic energy so that its pollutants are transformed into golden etheric atoms charged with effervescent life-force.

Yahoel ('Beauty of God')

One of the great angels, Yahoel guides the leaders of humanity. Pray to this mighty one if you are working to heal a political or environmental situation, which hangs on the making of wise decisions by those in positions of leadership and power.

Yahriel

Invoke this angel when you need to heal a condition locked in the subconscious. Yahriel holds dominion over the moon, who is queen of the subconscious realms. Yahriel works with the Virgin of Light, with Liromar, Angel of the Green Ray, and with Consonia, Angel of the Violet Ray.

Zadkiel

Zadkiel enfolds us in the inspiration of divine love as herald and angel of the new age.

He is known as the angel of benevolence, mercy, and memory; he is the angel of laughter and joy, and he is the angel of ascension.

Although Zadkiel is one of the angels of ultimate tenderness and protective enfoldment; he is also numbered among the ultimate Ka angels. He holds the secret of the violet flame, which has been described as 'a giant electrode of cosmic energy', and of which it is said that 'the use of the violet consuming flame is more valuable to humanity than all the wealth, all the gold and all the jewels of this planet.' The mystic presence of the violet flame within Zadkiel is his feminine consciousness. It is the point in his heart from which he can bestow the gift of miracles.

Zeruel ('Arm of God')

When you need to invoke the quality of strength of will, of body, of purpose, strength for the aura or the strength of courage, endurance and resilience, call on Zeruel, an angel 'set over strength'. Rampel and Zeruel work together. Rampel provides a repository for the strength you need, whilst Zeruel is its informing spirit. Rampel can be thought of as the spirit of passive strength; he stands firm, he guards the way, nothing can get past him. There is in him the monumental power of wholeness, completion, stillness. The sacred statement 'God rests' is associated with him. He stands in unassailable steadfastness, giving no quarter. Zeruel is the active potency of strength. When you need the motive power to carry yourself or some project or ideal forward, hitch yourself to Zeruel's chariot of fire.

Zlar

When you need spiritual insight and penetrative perception, call on this mighty being, 'one of the company of glorious and benevolent angels' who reveals secret wisdom.

Zoroel

Zoroel is a powerful healing angel, able to overcome the dominion of even the lordliest among the disease and pain elementals (entities that create and hold in place the etheric patterns and systems which bring into being, feed and perpetuate disease and pain). He has a heart that emanates miracles, like bright mirrors flashing.

Zuriel ('My Rock is God')

We can call on this prince of angels to help us overcome the mindsets and stumbling blocks that bar our way forward (to be brutally frank, Zuriel is known as a 'curer of the stupidity in man'!). We seek Zuriel's help in illuminating dim spiritual sight and opening spiritually deaf ears. Of course, we should always be careful to convey Zuriel's blessing as a free gift from the heart, rather than with the thought of replacing a person's individual viewpoint with our own. Zuriel belongs to the principalities, the order of angels who work miracles on earth.

List of Ka Angels

There follows a list of the Ka angels and their virtues for the sake of easy reference. However, it is important not to wander into the prison that has formed itself from our human tendency to list and catalogue! We are advised to think of limitlessness and an arena of wide open possibility when we think of angels. Worrying about names and getting facts right is not necessary and in fact would work against our communion with them. What is important is inner guidance, putting trust in our intuition. The following list, after all, is only a measure of how humans of antiquity have understood angels.

Their understanding is interesting and helpful, but it is even more interesting and helpful to form our own understanding and nurture our own vision of angels, even, perhaps, to formulate our own names for them! The best way to use this list might be as a springboard for your own appreciation of the Ka angels. The list is by no means exhaustive.

Alovar, Keyholder to the Treasury
Ambriel, Angel of Reflections
Anahita, Angel of Exalted Sexuality
Angels of Mercy (Transformative)
Azura, Angel of Tranquillity
Baglis, Angel of Temperance
Balthiel, Thwarter of Jealousy
Barbelo, Purveyor of Wisdom
Chalchiuhtlicue, the Purifier
Chamuel, Angel of Kindly Justice
Camaysar, Angel of the Marriage of Contraries
Charoum, Angel of Silence
Colopatiron, He Who Unlocks Prison Doors
Consonia, Mistress of the Subconscious
Derdekea, Angel of Salvation (also human)
Eistibus, Angel of Divination
Eleleth, the Brightener
Elemiah, Angel of Inner Journeying
Frankincense, Sweetener of Sorrow
Gabriel, Angel of Aspiration
Gavreel, the Peace-Maker
Haamiah, Angel of Truth
Hahaiah, Angel of Reconciliation
Haniel, Angel of Confidence
Haurvatat, Angel of Wholeness
Jophiel, Angel of Emancipation
Liromar, Angel of Emotional Healing
Mithra, Angel of Glory ('the Unconquerable Sun')
Melchior, Angel of Non-Judgment

Michael, Angel of Protection
Maion, Angel of Self-Discipline
Omniel, Angel of Unity
Phanuel, Angel of Forgiveness
Pathiel, Opener of the Way
Pedael, Angel of Deliverance
Peta Rose, Angel of Self-Worth
Pyrhea, Angel of the Primal Force
Rachmiel, Angel of Compassion
Rampel, Angel of Steadfastness and Resolution
Raphael, Angel of Healing and Integration
Sandalphon, Angel of the Earth
Shekinah, Angel of Unconditional Love
Shemael, Angel of Gratitude
Tabris, Angel of Free Will
Uriel, the Awakener
Valoel, Angel of Peace
Var Bahram, Angel of Victory
(The) Virgin of Light, Lamp-Bearer Sublime
(The) Virtues, Angels of Transformation
Vohu Manah, Angel of Good Thought
Vwyamus, Angel of Cleansing
Yahoel, Angel over World Leaders
Yahriel, Healer of Hidden Wounds
Zadkiel, Angel of Ascension
Zeruel, Angel of Strength
Zlar, Revealer of Wisdom
Zoroel, Healer of Pain
Zuriel, the Enlightener

We will find, as we enter deeply into working with the Ka angels, that it is possible to mix and match as far as angelic influences are concerned. We will also find that it is an angelic impulse or principle for new angels, previously unheard of, to arise out of our needs and as a response to our prayers. This spontaneous corporeality and metamorphosis is one of the many ways that the angels astonish us with the boundlessness of their loving and dedicated service.

Chapter Five

BROTHERS GRIMM

We have seen that the Ka angels are those that we can call on specifically in order to awaken from limitation and lethargy, and other components of the spiritual sleep that steals over our higher senses almost inevitably from time to time, as we seek to progress along our path. Once having been roused from sleep, we can request that the Ka angels keep us awake and, furthermore, that they deepen our awareness of the imprisoning grooves, self-sabotage and short-circuiting, which everyone tends to impose on themselves occasionally.

However, there is a story that needs to be told in order to heighten our understanding of the Ka angels and enrich our friendship and interaction with these noble beings prior to working directly with them. We have examined some aspects of this story already, but it is perhaps important to draw its disparate parts into a comprehensible whole. In truth, there are three stories, and this is the first, the one on which the others rest.

For me, the following narrative is directly, wholly, simply and literally true. Nevertheless, I do not wish to try to impose my own stance on anyone by suggesting too forcibly that it should be regarded as a reality, even though personally I find its reality undeniable. It would seem much wiser to suggest that its lineaments comprise a folk-tale, a creation of myth and dream; an offering, as it were, from the Brothers Grimm.

Let us say, as a preamble, that this world – the sphere of materialism – was created so that, through discernment, we could be born individually and consciously into a full realization of the reality of the spirit. Therefore, a tutelary split principle of darkness and light was brought about: being and non-being, the real and the illusory, right and wrong, offered to us as free choices throughout the course of our lives on this planet. Zoroaster called this split principle the Truth and the Lie. It brings great opportunities for spiritual enlightenment, and is therefore a good thing, and an expression of the will of God.

However, although it was right that this principle should be in place, something happened that was not God's plan. This is not to say, of course, that events took a turn beyond the reach of God's will. We know that such a thing is not possible, as God's will commands all. We can assume, perhaps, that it was right that the possibility of events transpiring as they did should exist; but the fact that what happened did actually happen went against the divine plan. In this case, instead of resisting it, human beings deliberately allied themselves with the Lie and sought to express its full potential within human consciousness. That full potential is, of course, complete annihilation and death everlasting. The plan of God afterwards adjusted so that everything would finally be brought into radiance and harmony, but nevertheless, the necessary – albeit natural and ineluctable – accommodation had to be made.

Here is the story.

There were two brothers who came to earth from a distant sphere to help with the divinely appointed task of establishing the essence of humanity on our planet.

They were known as the Serpent People, and they came with others of their exalted and kingly race. They were themselves king's sons, and their names were Enlil and Enki.

The queens of the Serpent People had a special significance: a royal mystery even deeper than that of the exalted kings. They carried within themselves the essence of the Mother, the great originating God. The Father existed within her and beside her in perfect equity, but it was acknowledged by the Serpent People that Mother God was the divine Source, for she had borne Father God from within the ineffable depths of herself. Therefore, the line of inheritance among the Serpent People was necessarily matriarchal.

According to this inviolable decree, Enki was due to succeed his father as king. Yet the father preferred Enlil. And so, against all established law, Enlil inherited.

What he inherited was a lawless conspiracy. His father Anu, the retired king who now held a form of presidency over the Serpent People on earth, had come to hate Mother God because things had gone wrong with their planetary mission. The earth people, according to plan, had been fostered into being. Taken from the essence of the Serpent People by means of their ova and sperm, they had been put into simian bodies via wondrous techniques belonging to both human and angelic consciousness. Simian people had thereafter gathered in communities on earth. (The Serpent People were humans of high degree and had a fully recognizable human form, but expressed certain subtle serpentine characteristics.)

To bring the simian people nearer to the lofty standard of the Serpent People, certain men had been chosen from among the ranks of the Serpent People, who were given the task of fathering children with human simian mothers.

This was done, but the resultant children were creatures of giant psychic ability and tall stature who used their enhanced powers to dominate others. They were known as the Naphidem. They indulged in savagery and cruelty to such a riotous extent that they had to be removed from the earth.

Although it was generally the masculine contingent among these offspring that had gone so badly off track, Anu, his son King Enlil, and others of their circle, blamed Mother God for decreeing that the simian people should be given Serpent People powers. The Serpent People were a much more advanced human race who took their name and the subtle aspects of their form from Mother God, for originally she was seen as a being of infinite light, an irradiating consciousness of ineffable fire generating all the stars of the universe, and who filled the abyss of space with her wave-esque potency of life. She was known as the Sacred Serpent, the Dragon Queen. Her keynote was all-encompassing love.

It was her law that all her human children, even those just starting out on the physical life-stream implanted within bodies of simian ancestry, should be given an equal chance to attain to the highest of the high. It was this law that King Enlil and his father decided that they definitely didn't like.

Allowing themselves to be thrown off-balance by the denseness and heaviness of earth and the challenge of the earthly forces, many of the Serpent People fell into a degree of blindness and error. All they could see was that the application of Mother God's law had brought chaos. They failed to understand the inevitable and inexorable movement of supernal love and the sacred principles of divine giving, justice and brotherhood that informed its motive force.

An unbalanced masculine ideal of superiority, repression and dominance seized them as they looked out in horror on a world where their own precious and lordly race had been lowered into animal bodies and had consequently behaved with worse than beastliness.

A small group of them, led by Anu and Enlil, decided that this new ideal, this wholly masculinized face in the mirror, was the true God: an all-masculine being who acted and thought like themselves, and who, like themselves, despised the Dragon Queen and wanted to see her perceptually crushed underfoot and held there in ignominy as punishment for her outrage, and as proof that her laws no longer had ascendancy over them.

They devised a plan to bring this about. It was called the Dolorous Blow, and, by black magic and foul ceremony of the most potent degree, they cut off the simian people's full conscious awareness of God, inevitably and simultaneously severing their own by the same act. (Of course, it was an impossibility to entirely deracinate it in either case.) Now the earthly humans had to struggle hard to conceive of God at all. When they did, it was easy to overlay their true apperception of God with the falseness of the new cruel ideation, even if Enlil and Anu only ever partially succeeded in such usurpation.

Their plot had matured into a coup, but it was only the beginning. The master plan of the conspirators was to get rid of physical manifestation altogether. Pride was their fall. They were the Serpent People. They existed in dimensions above that of the physical, material life, and they had no need of this new, experimental physical realm. They thought that it was disgusting and hateful, and any of their own who had expressed the lowliness to enter into it via a hated physical body was a pariah who should be eliminated and no longer allowed to contaminate the standing of their pure, superior race.

Enlil, with the help of Anu and a scientist of unprecedented genius, even created what is known as the Arrow of Time, whereby time points in a linear direction into the future in such a way that disorder follows order by inalienable decree. It was intended to bring about the inevitable death of the universe and put out all the stars. They saw the Dragon Queen now purely as mistress of the physical realm, and they thought that by destroying the universe they would destroy her forever. They wanted to eradicate entirely their connection to her and their knowledge that she was their divine source. This knowledge they called cursed and degenerate. They began to deny their own origins. They created the idea of a devil and a night-hag in her image, and stigmatized the serpent as an evil creature that deceived humanity.

Their concept of God was by now so corrupted that they believed that all this carnage and annihilation, this huge assault on the divine plan, was holy and God-directed. The idea of God as ravening tribal war-chieftain was born. And yet they were canny. They used this idea of God as male aggressor to stir unrest among the peoples of earth and to turn them against one another.

Yet it was only a very small contingent among the Serpent People who became thus deranged. Many of them were not swayed by Anu and Enlil's wrath and hatred. When the Dolorous Blow struck, it fell across their vision, too. They were confused and frightened. And yet they could not accept this new, remote, shadowy, conceptualized military leader as God. As the situation worsened, they fled from the higher planes, those spheres that were of earth and yet were more refined than the physical dimension of heavy matter and slow-spinning atoms. They left forever.

After causing much destruction on earth, Enlil and his cohorts were banished to a dreary and sinister astral realm connected to our planet. From here they strive to bring humanity under their control, and to fulfil their cherished plan of complete obliteration, not only of humanity and the planet, but of the entire material plane. They had evolved the horrible spiritual and scientific technology to do this. Yet cosmic law prevented them from such wholesale extermination. The only way to succeed was to connive and dupe and persuade hapless humanity, disconnected from its wisdom and from God, to destroy itself by its own hand and by its own will.

There was a small group of the Serpent People who were neither sucked into Anu and Enlil's conspiracy, nor confused by the fall of the Dolorous Blow. Enki and his consorts Nin-Khursag and Lilith headed this select assembly. They remained behind when the main body of the Serpent People took flight and left the planet, but they were not contained in an astral world similar to that inhabited by Enlil and his followers. The sphere where they dwelt, although similarly connected to the earth, was much more elevated, much more beautiful, being exquisitely refined and high-vibrational in quality.

They remained behind to help humanity – a simian humanity that they had initiated and blessed with their own essence – to overcome the terrible manipulations of Enlil. They had striven long and hard on humanity's behalf. They had ensured that it was given education and civilization, that it was instructed in the sacred mysteries and infused with spiritual enlightenment. These gifts were imparted against great odds, because Enlil fought them and their followers and obstructed their endeavours at every turn. The remotest concept of any refinements belonging to the Serpent People being bestowed on the earthlings was sheer anathema to him.

Enlil's idea had been to create ignorant slaves out of all of us very quickly, except for a chosen few who would become the 'master race'. The 'master race' would be allowed, through unspeakable experimentation on its hapless slaves, to create a biological technology that would actually be installed within the 'master race' itself at the cellular level. Once complete, this technology would enable the 'giant' race – the children of human simian mothers who had been fathered by men of the Serpent People and who were subsequently banished from earth – to return in triumph to the planet, entering into bodies specially prepared for them by the 'master race'.

They would then be free to exercise their hideous powers and fulfil their monstrous will to an unlimited extent, as, due to the black magical potency of the technology deployed, their banishment from earth could not be repeated. Because of the appalling reversal of cosmic laws that this situation would create, unprecedented disaster would be visited on the planet, and it, and its human cargo, would be destroyed forever ... despised earthly humanity, and its even more despicable mutant 'giant' race, gone eternally. Only such a 'final solution' could satisfy Enlil's benighted heart.

The influence of Enki, and all the great teachers and mystics of the light who followed him and gave forth his teachings, put paid to that idea, of course. But it has not prevented Enlil from continuing to seek to exert his will over us. He is prepared to take a longer course, a plan B, which appears to consist of a gradual wearing down of our resistance to his imposition of a blindness and insanity that, en masse, will lead us away from our glorious inheritance as spiritual beings and deliver us to the forces of chaos and destruction.

Enki and his colleagues, on the other hand, continued to see clearly how Father God and Mother God were combined in a perfect unity, with no inequality or imbalance in existence between them. They saw that Father God was, in his being and his consciousness, impossibly far removed from the ghostly, insubstantial and cosmically savage imposter that Enlil had created in his own image and superimposed on the planetary understanding of him.

Father God's joy in and reverence of Mother God became an underground stream of deeply sacred and secret knowledge that Enki guided through the centuries in its destiny of fated meanderings. These teachings included not only the correct understanding of the Father and the right note to sound in our human reverence of both aspects of Mother–Father God, but a third aspect – that of the heavenly Son–Daughter, the Divine Child who is expressed in creation and of whose essence we partake.

Some of these perfect teachings were included in the world's religions, both orthodox and obscure, but there was always a missing element. None of them entirely reconnected us with God as in the old days, when humanity had first been born into the care of the Serpent People. Surreptitious acts of spiritual sabotage were purposely seeded into theological doctrines. Through much manipulation and subversive spiritual influence, Enlil managed to maintain us in our ignorance so that only ever a sparse number of individuals, able to take a remarkable leap, managed to reconnect.

It was Enki's great mission, first through Zoroaster and many other spiritual luminaries, and ultimately through the Christ, whose teachings have been obscured but who spoke through the perfect combined vessel of Jesus and Mary Magdalene, to overturn Enlil's ill-willed rule and liberate us forever.

As well as the great spiritual teachers and masters who were part of the flow of Enki's spiritual underground stream, there gathered a mighty company of angels to help his cause. Chief of these, of course, was Archangel Michael, but there were and are many of great spiritual magnitude. They comprise, in particular, the angels who are ready to offer their help as Ka angels. They know that there is a corner to be turned, now, in our own times, and that it is imperative that we turn it together. They know that many of us have fallen into something of a defile or a slough, and that the fact that we should have done so was almost una-voidable. They also know that, with their help, we will arise victorious, perhaps to greater heights of strength than if we had never foundered and sunk.

They come now, as of old, as if in a great column, offering the hand of joy and friendship to us.

Chapter Six
THE GUARDIAN ANGEL

It is essential to connect with the Ka angels via the guardian angel.[1] This process is crucial for the establishment of safety and harmony in our dealings with the Ka angels. When we invite them into our lives, it is imperative that their vital energy and the shining dynamics of their consciousness should blend with our own on rays of wisdom and correct resonance in order to address the golden vistas of aspiration and the healing of deep-seated problems that comprise the compass of their service to us.

Sometimes, people tend to think of their guardian angel in terms of an angelic group, or believe that a relative who has passed over has become their guardian angel. Human spirits assuredly do work with the guardian angel to offer protection to a loved one, and it is true that our angel friends gather in groups around us to inspire and protect us. Nevertheless, I believe that the guardian angel is not human, or one of a group of angels, but that it is a single entity assigned to each individual human being. It stands beside our personal guide, an advanced human spirit who is allied to every soul coming into incarnation on earth.

Each of us has many guides and many angels in attendance as we walk our path through life, but these two, the

---

1 The instructions given in this chapter can also be found in my book, *Your Guardian Angel*, Watkins, 2007

main guide and the guardian angel allotted to every human being, are the supreme two sources of guidance and guardianship – the guardian angel at our left-hand side, and the guide at our right.

A rhyme from esoteric lore tells us:

> Our guardian angel and gentle guide,
> On every narrow path and wide,
> Walk ever-faithful by our side.

Both our guide and our guardian angel will help us to attune safely to the Ka angels.

The guardian angel in particular has an important part to play in facilitating our connection with our divine source, especially regarding issues of protection and purification. There are many wonderful advantages that will reward the development of our awareness of this shining being that walks by our side and, simultaneously, stands behind us and enfolds us in the great circle of its sweeping wings.

Life lived in conscious communion with our guardian angel is a life enriched and enhanced beyond measure. However, we do need to build our relationship with our guardian. Some people believe that we come into incarnation with this relationship already in place, but in my experience this is not so. A fundamental relationship already exists, but it is an unconscious one. It is a part of the purpose of human life on earth to develop a conscious relationship with our guardian angel, so earthing the divine into common experience, and thus transforming our lives and our destiny, on both an individual and a global scale.

A description of my own guardian angel might be of

interest. It appears in beautiful swathes of colour above my bed each night. It is difficult to convey the loveliness of these colours; imagine looking through the clearest, most beautifully tranquil water or liquid crystal as a speculum through which the colours appear, as if they are contained in a sanctified lake of the most perfect, angelic translucency. These colours pulsate and ripple and become more potent as they are observed, like a delight deepening. They appear actually to have substance, as if each were a swirling curtain of a glorious and refined material which is the colour itself, like the northern lights.

My angel has fields of energy that both look and waft like great wings hovering over me. Its colours are always the same, but if I happen to be working on a certain problem or project, other colours sometimes occur. Lately, and for some time, a vividly bright lime green has come into play which manifested only rarely in the past. If my angel doesn't come to me of its own volition, I call it or 'summon' it, and thereafter it appears (just occasionally it declines; I am not sure why). Its main colour is amethyst deepening into violet, and I often catch a glimpse of that colour, or of the bright lime green (emanating from an immaterial source), during the day. This is my sign that my guardian angel is responding to my conscious awareness of its presence. The oddest aspect about my guardian angel is that I can study it closely with my physical eyes, just as anyone might scrutinize any observable phenomenon, but, if I close them, I continue to see the angel just as well.

One of the many magical and poetic aspects of angel communication is that their language is a language of colour. They speak to us not only in words and in symbols, but especially in colours, communing with us through every differing hue, although angelic colours always shine with a wondrous diamond clarity, radiant and transparent as if they are lit by an inner light. They have a clear, calm lustre and are never muddy, brash, overcharged or heavy.

As your relationship with your own guardian angel develops, you will become aware of its colour or colours, and these will give an indication of what your angel is saying to you – its great theme and plan for your life – entrusted to it before you came into incarnation by your higher self, your spiritual aspect that never leaves the supernal worlds and which is in perfect accord with your angel. This, in turn, points to the colour ray to which you are attuned, which develops the message further. Each one of us comes into being under the influence of one or more of the seven great rays of creation, whose essence and mystery are reflected in the lovely and ethereal manifestation of the rainbow.

The Breath

We communicate with our guardian angel via our breath – through air. We need to breathe gently and a little more deeply than usual when preparing to commune with our angel. Our guardian angel connects us to other angels whose assistance we need, and helps to shine their qualities into our soul through the magical power of our breath. It will wire us to the Ka angels with a consummate skill that ensures our perfect safety and security.

Angels enter into us through the medium of air, the supreme symbol of brotherhood; for we all breathe the same air. Do angels breathe? They do; but their respiration draws on the refined spiritual essence of the element of air – what air is, we might say, before it is lowered in vibration and becomes mundane, physical and corruptible.

It is of benefit to take the time to be still and to dwell on our breathing as a sacred act. Mary Magdalene's gospel tells us, 'Those that listen will hear the breath of Silence.'

When we practise sacred breathing, we listen to the rhythm of our breath; this draws us gently into the Silence, that point of peace within the heart that is the threshold of the spiritual worlds.

A beautiful and ancient Sanskrit mantra is 'Ham Sah'. This intonation imitates the sound of the in-breath and the out-breath. 'Ham' is spoken as you breathe in, and comprises the affirmation 'I Am'. 'Sah' is spoken as you breathe out, and means the sacred flame in the heart, the 'nous', the Divine Spark – our spiritual reality, which is our true self.

A Simple Breathing Exercise

The wonderful healing art of the guardian angel is evident in a simple breathing exercise that can be combined with the one described above, or can be practised separately.

As you breathe in, collect together all your fears, frets, hassles and anxieties. Hold the breath a moment, and see these swirling negativities contained in a transparent blue sphere. Breathe out all your worries as if you were emptying the sphere into the arms of your angel. He or she will take them all from you, and gently bear them away. Breathe in again, and this time, see the blue sphere fill with sunshine and happiness.

Breathe out, and feel the peace of the joyful sunshine wash over you.

Let the blue sphere become a kite with a string within the firm grasp of your hands. Now let the blue spherical kite ascend into the heavens, taking your consciousness with it so that you are in heaven while still firmly grounded on earth. This simple and effortless exercise will help you to prepare and purify your chakras before connecting with the Ka angels.

The Chakras

Our seven main chakras are the base chakra, at the base of the spine; our sacral chakra, just below the navel; our solar plexus chakra; our heart chakra; our throat chakra, in the hollow of the throat; our brow chakra, on the ridge of our brow, between the eyes; and our double crown chakra, one of which corresponds with our crown and is seated in the middle of the brain, the other being situated at the top of the forehead, in the centre.

Although our Guardian Angel will use other chakras to communicate with us, especially the throat chakra, initial contact is always made via the heart.

To draw closer to your guardian angel, and to discover which of your chakras it prefers to use in its communion with you, you can use a short and simple dedication ceremony, which I have set out below. The ceremony will lead you to discover not only the main chakra or chakras through which it prefers to communicate with you, but also the colour or colours with which your angel resonates. To help this process (it is not always necessary), you might like to hold a sheet of pure white paper in your hands as you perform the ceremony. When you ask your guardian angel to give you its colour, gently gaze at the centre of the paper. Take care not to stare or strain your eyes; just let your vision softly rest on the paper. The colour of the angel will be subtly reflected onto its surface. You may, of course, prefer not to use the paper, and to use your inner sight only.

Because this is a ceremony dedicated to your guardian angel, light a white candle in honour of your angel, if possible, before you begin.

Dedication Ceremony to Your Guardian Angel

Be still, and open your heart to the Divine Presence.

Within your heart is a perfect six-pointed Star, shining with a holy light.

Look deep into the centre of this peacefully shining star.

See, in the heart of the Star, a radiant angel form with wings of light outstretched, indescribably brilliant, so calm and still, remote from the material plane, yet all love.

Say in your heart, 'I request and accept the love, the guidance and the service of my guardian angel, and of all my angel friends.'

The Angel of the Star greets you with a glad welcome and enfolds you in its great wings. From its shining heart, your guardian angel takes flight toward you.

You are accepted into the Brotherhood of Angels and Humanity.

Three gifts are given to you by the angel. They are:

a colour … accept it, remember it;
a light touch on one of your chakras …
remember which one
an image or a sign … what is it?

The guardian angel speaks: 'Wherever you walk, you will be enfolded in my wings and accompanied by angels. Be at peace. All is well. Amen.'

Close the ceremony by blowing out the candle, aware as you do so that your breath is holy and can give forth blessings, and send your love and thanks to your angel.

Now you have drawn close to your guardian angel you will find that the lines of communication between you remain beautifully alive and vibrant. From this point on, you need only call on your guardian angel and request that it links you to the Ka angels in safety and harmony each time, before proceeding to work with them.

At the same time, it is a good idea to request help from your guide. You can make contact with your guide by adapting the ceremony given above. Enact it in just the same way as for your guardian angel, but replace the references to it and to the angels in each case with wording appropriate to connecting with your guide. Some of the references to the angels, rather than being reworded, can be left out altogether. It is very likely that you will be surprised and delighted by your heart encounter with your guardian angel and your guide.

Each time before beginning work with the Ka angels, you might say:

> My dear guardian angel, my dear guide, please
>   be with me as I seek to work with the
>   highest angelic forces.
> Link me safely and securely to these great ones.
>   I ask that you harmonize and facilitate our
>   communion, and bless its outcome with the
>   heavenly gift of spiritual gold.
> I offer my thanks to you both and move
>   forward with you both, my guide on my
>   right, my guardian angel on my left.'

I have been asked whether it is necessary to pepper our addresses to the angels and those who help us from the spiritual realms with terms of endearment. It is not strictly necessary if they make you feel uncomfortable, but on the other hand, these transactions are transactions of love, and it is appropriate that they should be expressed as such.

Your guide will not only join forces with your guardian angel in affording you protection during your encounters with the Ka angels, but will also actively facilitate your conscious experience of them and with them, and bless that experience with the greatest felicity that can be granted to your mutual communion.

Chapter Seven
THUS SPAKE ZARATHUSTRA

The title above is the title of the core of Nietzsche's great philosophical works[2]. Nietzsche has a bearing on Enki's story and on the Ka angels, which is vital to consider. And Nietzsche's story in itself is astonishing.

Friedrich Wilhelm Nietzsche was born on 15 October 1844 in eastern Germany. Astrologers will note that he was a Libran, the only sign of the zodiac to be represented by an inanimate object, because of course Libra's emblem is the heavenly scales, the symbol of balance. This is worth bearing in mind! It is also to be noted that we are still in Brothers Grimm territory concerning Nietzsche's birthplace and era, because it was about this time that the intrepid brothers set out to collect the ancient folklore of the majestic and mysterious German forests.

Strangely enough, and therefore significantly, Nietzsche was born fewer than 30 miles from Wittenberg, the town where Martin Luther began his great Protestant Reformation by nailing to the door of Wittenberg's church his 95 theses. Protestantism is considered by some scholars to be the vestigial remains of what was once the great Cathar heresy. To clarify the courage and resolution of Martin Luther and

---

2 The anecdotes pertaining to Nietzsche, plus quotes, are from an abridged transcript of *Jung's Seminar on Nietzsche's Zarathustra* edited by James L. Jarrett, published by Princeton University Press in 1998. Jung borrowed from Nietzsche's correspondence and diary entries.

his vision, previous nailings to church doors throughout Europe often consisted of the flayed human skin of heretics who had been skinned alive for their presumption in refusing to believe, in literal and unwavering terms, the doctrines of the Holy Mother Church.

Nietzsche's father was a pastor who personally conducted the baptismal rites for his new-born son. Again, destiny unveiled herself. His father posed a question around which to deliver his sermon: 'What will be the fate of this child? Will it be good, or will it be evil?' A vexed question, indeed, for Nietzsche seemed to bring an uprush of both good and evil into the world via his famous body of philosophy. He said of himself:

> I know my fate. One day there will be associated with my name the recollection of something frightful – of a crisis like no other before on earth, of the profoundest collision of conscience, of a decision evoked against everything that until then had been believed in, demanded, sanctified.
>
> I am not a man. I am dynamite.'

His words arose from a prophetic vision, because nothing during most of his lifetime indicated that he would achieve renown. He had to leave his professorial post at the University of Basel after ten years due to ill health. His constitution was so weakened by illnesses contracted in his youth that he was forced to spend 36 hours in bed for every fortnight or so that he spent working on his books. His marriage proposals were met with rejection, his students deserted him, his friends withdrew their support, his book sales dwindled to almost nothing. The first three parts of his masterpiece sold abysmally on initial release – between 60 and 70 copies each. In order to publish the fourth and final part, he was obliged to meet the costs himself, and was able to pay for the issue of a mere 40 copies.

He wrote another seven books, and then fell into a decline. He was cared for by his mother and his sister for the last ten years of his life, silent and helpless, seemingly unaware of his surroundings as if in a deep trance. He died of a stroke as the century turned. He was only 55 years old.

And yet he was visited by astounding visions and flights of genius. He wrote in a lyrical prose comparable to the finest in the German language. His philosophy is disturbing, often sinister, and yet marvellous. In the folk-tale called 'The Demon Lover', the bridegroom shows his bride two bright hills from the deck of their onward-plunging ship. One is heaven and one is hell. All hangs on the choices they have made as to where they are bound. The story serves as a dramatization of the dynamics of his thinking as it relates to the human psyche and the destiny of the soul.

Nietzsche began his university career as a committed and inspired Christian. He had been labelled 'the little minister' at school because of his avid study of the Bible. His focus and his dream were to follow in his father's footsteps. At university he began to read the poets, the novelists, the philosophers and the thinkers who embraced the ideal of German Romanticism with its high heroics, immersing himself in the music of composers who expressed its spirit. Its counterweight was Enlightenment, an older, more sober movement which endorsed reason, order, science, measured restraint, the acquisition of studious knowledge and the clear, cool observations of the intellect over mysticism and individualism. One espoused heart over head, the other head over heart. Nietzsche was definitely in favour of the first doctrine.

Shortly before Nietzsche started his first year at university, Darwin published his work *On the Origin of Species*. This book sparked searching debate, and by the end of the academic year Nietzsche had lost his religious convictions and thrown over his theological studies to concentrate entirely on classical philology.

After the loss of his faith, the discovery of Schopenhauer's dark broodings alerted Nietzsche to some resonance deep within himself. Schopenhauer's stance proclaims that there is no meaning to life whatsoever, and that though it were better not to be born at all, if, tragically, the misfortune of life does happen to impose itself, one should at least try to ensure that one ended the pointless affair as soon as possible. This strange philosophy of despair gripped Nietzsche dramatically. He had come upon the works of the mournful philosopher in a bookshop, and stood mesmerized, feeling as if the dour old man had taken shape out of the shadows. 'It seemed as if Schopenhauer were addressing me personally,' he wrote afterwards. 'I felt his enthusiasm, and seemed to see him before me.' Nietzsche's vessel of imagination was vivid, evocative, passionate and theatrical.

It seems that the dark manipulative forces, seeing that he hung in the balance, used this vessel to connect him with a fellow traveller in philosophy who had been overcome by them.

It was within the same period that he rushed out of the gala first night opening of Wagner's opera house in Bayreuth and dramatically vomited in public. The reaction was not due to any physical cause. It has been suggested that it was because he recognized Wagner's flaws as a composer, despite being a devoted fan and a personal friend of the musician. Yet such a reaction is an acknowledged symptom, not only of recognizing a soul danger, but, on having it foisted deep into you, of rejecting the contamination through violent regurgitation.

Nietzsche read, thought, acted, lived and formulated his philosophical works with all the intensity and passion of his soul. I believe that, Brothers-Grimm-like, something sinister winged its way into his heart that night, something living and conscious that had attached itself energetically to Wagner's music. Because Nietzsche's psyche was so open, because his soul was so sensitive, his genius so emotionally fluid and, most of all, because a profound morbidity had taken hold in his heart, something assaulted him by seeking to take over his inner citadel. It was responding to his poetic genius, because it could feed on it. But it was not benign. On that occasion, Nietzsche expelled it in full. When it happened again, he was only partially successful.

It happened one beautiful morning when he had retreated to the Alps. A figure had been appearing to him in dreams for some time. He must have felt its presence draw near as he set out from the little Swiss mountain village of Sils-Maria that nestled in the valley. He wrote of it afterwards:

> I emerged into the morning air. I was greeted by the most beautiful day the Upper Engadine had ever disclosed to me – clear, glowing with colour, and including all the contrasts and all the intermediary gradations between ice and the south.'

By 'ice and the south' (that is, above and below), Nietzsche draws attention to the contrasts whose mysteries had fuelled him all his life, since as a babe-in-arms his father had bowed over him and asked the waiting congregation, 'Will this child be good, or evil?' The resolution of duality had been his great quest. Holding the Libran point of balance and invested with his individual genius, he had the power within him to heal the division between the two. He always said that his mission was to rise to a height 'beyond good and evil'. It gave him a love for the mountain tops, even for the icy conditions that obtained thereon. He felt their punishment, yet revelled in their purity.

However, it is clear that he associates the purity and power of the mountain heights with the upward thrust and drive of masculinity. His understanding of womanhood was not exemplary. He distrusted women. And here we find him, on this morning that will change the world, climbing up from the valley:

> The Valley Spirit never dies.
> It is called the Mysterious Female.
> And the doorway of the Mysterious Female
> Is the base from which heaven and earth
>   spring.
> It is there within us all the time.
> Draw upon it as you will, it never runs dry.

So said Lao-tzu, the ancient Chinese mystic, in his *Tao Te Ching*. He, unlike Nietzsche, was attuned to the Sacred Feminine.

And in the valley lay the village of Sils-Maria, the place of the Divine Mother.

This is the verse that Nietzsche composed that day–his song to the world to convey what happened. A spirit, an essence, a soul-shape passed into him, and became one with him.

I sat there waiting – not for anything.

Beyond good and evil, enjoying now the light
Now the shade, now only play, now
The lake, now the noon, wholly time without
 end.
Then, suddenly, friend, one became two –
And Zarathustra passed me by.

He now began to write his masterpiece in earnest. It took him only ten days apiece to compose the first three parts – a staggering achievement. And into it he poured this culmination of inspired movement of thought that had come to him on the mountain, like a symphony. He entitled the work *Thus Spake Zarathustra*, and in it the voice of the ancient Persian mystic spoke anew, through him. It was as if he channelled the spirit of Zarathustra. Throughout the work, he almost literally makes this claim.

And the work speaks of passing beyond good and evil. It cites compassion as an inexcusable weakness. It proclaims that God and associated naïve ideas that an afterlife exists are finished with; religions are empty husks without nourishment that are making ready to be gone with the wind. The Christian God is a concept that can no longer contain the highest aspirations and ideals of western civilization, which must now be freed from the restriction and burden of such limitation. History demands an entirely new ethical system that is not built upon faith, but reaches beyond our narrow concepts of good and evil. Our individual aspiration is what, above all else, should fuel us. And our highest aspiration should be to transcend ourselves, to lift ourselves onto the next rung of our personal evolution. We should strive to overcome our animal nature and reach upward to attain the crown of that higher evolution, which is absorption into the super-human. We should, in fact, be fired by no other ideal than to become super-human.

Nietzsche says: 'Man is a rope stretched between the animal and the Superman – a rope over an abyss.' He then goes on to whisper intimations of the abyss: 'What is good? Everything that heightens the feeling of power in man, the will to power, power itself. What is bad? Everything that is born of weakness.'

At this point in history, after the Nazi horror, we are more likely to observe at once that considering its own power without regard to anything else is exactly what the animal does, and what our own animal nature would tempt us to do. And it is interesting, and chastening, to consider that all the iconic 'Superman' heroes, born from this rant, have suffered misfortune, crippling, and death, as if from a curse. Yet, seen from a long-range perspective it is not a curse, but an intrinsic teaching, which points out very clearly that there is something seriously wrong with our vision of Superman when we view him from Nietzsche's angle, because his is the viewpoint of the abyss.

For instance, he seems to forget that from our greatest weakness, our greatest strength is born. And it comes forth as a mighty but gentle strength, unconquerable but kindly and humane, understanding as it does within its very roots the vulnerability and suffering of the weakness from which it grew. We might see this truth as a reflection of the wisdom of Christ compared to the ignorance of the Shadow or, as Zoroaster called it, the Lie.

And yet there are also such glimmers of bright truth in Nietzsche's vision. It is as if the distant peaks of his perception shine with a pure light, but the terrain across which he directs us to reach them is a steaming, treacherous bog.

Because, if we do as Nietzsche directs, if we place our personal power before any other consideration and regard vital aspects of human goodness such as compassion in the light of culpable weakness, then we evoke not our superhuman self, but the Beast itself, which rises from the abyss to devour us. And, historically, that is exactly what we proceeded to do.

There is another way to interpret Nietzsche's insights, of course. We can choose the bright hill of heaven rather than the bright hill of hell. Nevertheless, the way forward is not contained in Nietzsche's work, but only the far-distant towering peaks of a great truth, resplendent in the glory of what we can become; what the world can become.

There is no doubt that Hitler was fired and enthused by Nietzsche's masterpiece. The whole of the Nazi ideology is encompassed in the hellish interpretation of his Superman vision. Had it not been so wholly and perfectly espoused, would Hitler's own vision have been less sure? Would his insidious grip have been less unrelenting, his convictions less confident? Would his hypnotic allure have been weaker? My feeling is that they would.

Hitler revered Nietzsche as a national hero, and visited his home, which Nietzsche's sister Elizabeth had turned into a museum after his death. He probably first read Nietzsche as a conscript in the First World War, when 150,000 copies of *Thus Spake Zarathustra* were handed out by the German government, together with the Bible, as inspirational reading for the troops.

Had that same lurid, dangerous potency that leapt into Nietzsche's innermost being, first unsuccessfully through Wagner, and then more victoriously through the spirit on the mountain, shone its strange consuming light into

Hitler's soul and made those pathological dimensions its abode? Hitler had a dream one night in the trenches that a great wall of suffocating mud, tsunami-high, was bearing down on him and on all that he could see. It awoke him, and he left his position to get some air. Seconds later, the trench was blown up and his comrades died in the asphyxiating wall of mud created by its collapsing walls, just as he had seen in his dream. It was at that moment he decided that fate had singled him out to save his country and sweep it to unprecedented glory. His mission began that night.

And yet, Nietzsche hated anti-Semitism and nationalism. One of his last acts, before he retreated into decline and self-isolation, was to throw his arms protectively around a horse in the street that had been beaten to its knees by a heartless carter, to save it from further blows. And yet he professed to despise compassion as a 'weakness'. He took the conundrum that was his nature and his life with him into the darkness and silence of his final years, unharmonized and unresolved, as was the problem of the duality with which he had struggled throughout his time on earth.

Nietzsche had said of his meeting upon the mountain that it was Zarathustra who came to him. The ancient Persian mage had explained that he had come to set right a terrible mistake he had made thousands of years ago. His error, the gravest in human history, was the invention of morality. He charged Nietzsche with the solemn task of righting this wrong he had committed against humanity. He, Zarathustra, would point the way forward. Nietzsche said of this process, 'One hears – one does not see; one takes, one does not ask who gives; … I have never had any choice in the matter.'

'*Da … wurde eins zu zwei – und Zarathustra ging an mir vorbei*'… 'One became two and Zarathustra passed me by,' Nietzsche had declared in his poem 'Sils-Maria'; Zarathustra, who was the spiritual son of Enki, whose teachings of light, often secretly, had informed humanity's faltering steps from the beginning of our present civilization; Zarathustra, who came with knowledge of angels, and whose understanding of these bright beings of blessing and benevolence is our own today; Zarathustra, whose illumination culminated in the light of the cosmic Christ. Was it really he who had come to Nietzsche on the mountain?

I think that it was. But he was not alone. His space was contested. Let us see who might also have come to Nietzsche that day.

Chapter Eight
ENKI'S OTHER SON

As we have seen, the biblical Ham was the first Zoroaster or Zarathustra. Others succeeded him, but he was the original dispenser of the teachings of Enki, or Ahura Mazda, God of Light. Enki was in fact a human being, but a human being so evolved that to humans living in physical bodies at the material level of life he seemed godlike. He also embraced the Christ principle, the cosmic spirit greater than universes, known as the Third Principle of God who oversees our evolution into beings of limitless light.

Laurence Gardner, who was given access to the Duke of Albany's very ancient archives, which have never been made available to the public arena, researched the identity and ancestry of Ham with scholarly thoroughness. He gives strong evidence to the effect that Cain was the ancestor of the Magian priestly dynasts descending throughout several centuries BC whose titular name was Zarathustra. The originator of this Persian succession, which had its roots in Sumerian Chaldea, was the biblical Ham, known as Chem-Zarathustra. Cain was Ham's many-generations-distant grandfather.

Cain and his descendants were closely linked with Enki, because Cain was Enki's son. This family was entrusted with profound alchemical secrets. When the line reached Ham (Zarathustra), a deeply gifted and spiritually attuned individual, there was a culmination in his soul of the teachings of the Temple of Enki. They became newly forged, brought to an unprecedented level of perfection.

Enki chose this descendant, Zarathustra, as he who would convey the flowering of these teachings to the world. His spiritual refinement and genius of insight made him the perfect repository and dispenser of the secrets of the Temple of Enki and Nin-Khursag, or the Temple of John.

From the point of his initiation into the deepest rites of the inner temple, bestowed on him personally by Nin-Khursag and Enki, Zarathustra became 'Chem-Zarathustra'—'Chem' indicating the Sacred Goat, was the Goat of Capricorn. We know the mysteries of Capricorn better today by the symbol of the unicorn, the one-horned horse: bright white, pure of spirit and fleet-footed, whom old texts describe as inhabiting 'the high places', the mountain tops of life and of soul aspiration. In the mysterious star temple of Glastonbury, where the zodiacal signs are delineated by natural features of the landscape, Capricorn is symbolized by a unicorn.

The goat and the unicorn become one when the goat is cast in sacred mode. They both scale rocky heights. In mundane actuality (always an objectification and an expression of deeper truths), the sure-footed goat can climb the highest and the most difficult mountain terrain. This is why it is the emblem of Capricorn. The oldest sources quote Capricorn as the Sea-Goat. There is perfect symbolism in this image, depicting the creature born of the primal sea that ascends to the loftiest mountain peaks of spiritual realization.

Zarathustra's knowledge, its adherents always contested and persecuted, culminated in the teachings of the Christ, visited by the Magi, who passed on their symbols to him at birth as a sign that he was the one designated to carry them forward.

The Magi, associated with serpent wisdom, comprised the priesthood of the Temple of Enki/Oannes/John, whose earthly leader was Ham or Zarathustra. The secrets of the Christ, some removed from the Gospels, some overlaid by obscurity, and some actually arriving on earth after his ascension, were protected by clandestine brotherhoods such as a secret, inner component of the Magi priestly caste, the Brotherhood of the Children of Solomon, and, as a descendant of these, the Knights Templar, who venerated the Sacred Goat as the symbol of the highest movement of aspiration towards spiritual attainment.

But there is a most mysterious secret connected with the Sacred Goat. We will look at this later, as it is one of the untold stories previously mentioned. For now, it is perhaps sufficient to know that the Sacred Goat enshrined within itself a point of mystical knowledge of a magnitude and depth that the human mind in its mundane state can barely conceive of. This ineffable point is the Khem or the Chem, the uttermost essence of the Sacred Goat. Its emanation, its mystery, its treasure beyond price, was the knowledge of alchemy (al-chem-y), the science of the All-Knowing. Its wondrous promise was the overcoming of the darkness, or changing dross matter into gold.

Attaining the Chem was to make a huge evolutionary stride out into the stars. The mundane view of life was put aside forever, for the Chem was God-consciousness, profound awareness of God. 'Ram' was higher knowledge symbolized by the sacrificial sheep, but Chem was an even greater state of knowing, symbolized by the sacrificial goat. Later, because Enki's teachings were reviled and certain contingencies sought to cast odium on them, the goat was denigrated. But it always had this deep, secret meaning, recognized by initiates.

Both Ram and Chem knowledge were associated with Enki, the heights he attained and the initiatory knowledge he bestowed, and were later associated with the Golden Fleece (the putting on or assumption of divine knowledge) won by Jason and the Argonauts.

Ham was a later term for this Chem knowledge, although, as we see from the word 'alchemy', which gave birth to 'chemistry' when the modern discipline displaced the ancient, the older term was the one that survived. (We see the later term being applied to Avram or Abram, for instance, when, after initiation, he became Abra-ham.) 'Ham' is an earlier form of 'Hermes', a Greek rendition whose root is in *herma*, an esoteric reference to a specially constructed 'pile of stones', which relates to the creation of the pyramids. In Sanskrit, a language that developed from the very ancient Chaldean tongue originating from the earliest Sumerian cuneiform, which was Ham's own, the word 'Ham' equates with the sacred 'I Am'.

It was Ham or Hermes who encountered the golden serpent or dragon Poimandres in the Mesopotamian desert and converted the teachings of Poimandres into the wisdom of Zoroastrianism. Poimandres was a manifestation of Enki and Nin-Khursag, who was known to the Babylonians as Oannes and later as John.

Enlil was Enki's brother. Perpetrator of many dark deeds, he usurped the kingship from Enki and planned the destruction of humanity and planet earth. He embraced the dark principle, the cosmic destroyer. This being is in some ways not a real being at all, but a reversed principle activated by a mighty angel whose mission is to help humanity to develop consciousness of the light and to express ultimate strength and steadfastness in that consciousness by the force of opposition or contrast.

The true reality of the divine life lies far beyond and above such duality, as Nietzsche saw so clearly. The angel is sanctioned by God and has a righteous purpose, but the idea is to resist his adversarial power, not to wholeheartedly embrace it, as poor, foolish Enlil did. To keep humanity and the earth alive and progressing, Enki had to make sure that he was always one step ahead of his evil-intentioned brother.

But Enlil did not work alone. Anu, his presidential father, headed the original conspiracy to destroy humankind, but he tended to be in and out of affairs on earth, and was absent from the planet for long stretches of time. Eventually, Enlil commanded not only the Serpent People and the earthlings they oversaw, but the conspiracy itself.

In order to further his schemes, he enlisted the help of one we know from ancient history as Marduk. He was the fierce and unforgiving god of Babylon, a city-state that arose after the terrible destruction of Ur in Sumer. Marduk was taken to the royal palace and groomed from a very early age to partake in Enlil's plans. He was exposed to horrible rites that gave him certain powers.

Marduk was one of the dreaded Naphidem, the last of the race that had come forth as sons and daughters of human simian mothers and Serpent People fathers and had despoiled the earth with their abhorrent behaviour. He, however, appeared to behave himself. He was, after all, Enki's son; Enki had been among those of the Serpent People males selected to impregnate the chosen earth women, and Marduk was the result.

Enki had no idea in those early years of exactly what Anu and Enlil were up to. He knew about their plot from the beginning, but initially he could not foresee the lengths to which they would go, not only to implement it, but also to undermine and dishonour him.

As far as he understood, Marduk had been specially chosen by Anu and Enlil, and was in receipt of royal favours in the arena of education, training and decorum. Later, when the Naphidem were banished from the earth, Marduk remained in El-Elyon's (Enlil's) court. Enki thought he had been excused his fate because he was innocent. In fact, the specialized rites to which Marduk had been subjected gave him the power to remain on earth.

It was Marduk who struck the Dolorous Blow. There was a feminine influence from the consorts of both Anu and Enlil that, against their will, stayed their hand against this cosmic crime. Marduk was entirely free from feminine influence and, moreover, was chafing at the bit to perpetrate the dreadful deed … The Dragon Queen had had the gall to imprison his people, the Naphidem, in a dreamy astral dimension where they could not enact their desires in any but the most unsatisfactorily vague, unreal and inchoate way, like an old man's drifting and disappearing daydream winding down into sleep. It was an outrage! All of his psychopathic tendencies cried out to immerse himself in the desecration of the Dolorous Blow. His name afterwards became Marduk the Avenger. It was a title bestowed on him with flattery and false courtesy by Enlil and Anu to encourage his enthusiasm for the crime.

Enlil worked with him, but was always the commander-in-chief. They despised one another, and yet were colleagues.

As far as Enlil was concerned, the Naphidem, locked away into an astral dimension where they could only dream of the physical realities they once enjoyed on earth and yearn for the day when they could experience them again, must also be eliminated.

Marduk was his guarantee that they would one day be brought forth from their astral prison and re-colonize the earth, because that was Marduk's whole aim and aspiration. He had been promised kingship over them, once they had returned, by Anu and Enlil. Both men detested Marduk and held him in the deepest contempt. As far as they were concerned, he was the source of their profoundest shame, for the Naphidem were half Serpent People, half human simian; they were, in effect, contaminated Serpent People. Anu and Enlil's plan accommodated the extermination of the Naphidem alongside the extermination of the planet and its humanity. They all had to go, and Marduk himself would activate the whole process; for, by breaking cosmic law in the way that Enlil and Anu knew the Naphidem inevitably would once they were released, they would set in motion the answering law that would bring wholesale destruction to the planet. Job done.

Marduk was kept entirely ignorant of this final stage of their plan, of course. As far as he knew, Anu and Enlil simply wanted to free themselves from the yoke of the Dragon Queen and assert male authority and dominance in its place. In breaking her power, as Marduk saw it, the Naphidem would also be freed from it, and could come back to earth for all the blood-letting and horror that they enjoyed best. It was a wonderful plan, and he diligently applied himself to its fulfilment. Nevertheless, he felt uneasy, and the presence of Enlil, either immediate or indirect, absolutely terrified him. His soul caught intimations of that from which his mind was kept in ignorance, and shuddered. His hatred for Enlil smouldered.

One of the earlier attempts to release the Naphidem back onto the earth occurred in 1960 BC. The Tower of Babel had been built after the city in which the Temple of Enki was situated was seized by Enlil, and the powers of the Temple, which preserved a modicum of the power that once connected the earth and her humanity directly to God, were unlawfully directed into this great tower whose construction was ordered ostensibly by Marduk, but actually by Enlil. The tower was for the purpose of releasing the Naphidem hordes back onto earth via an abusive use of the connective powers of Enki's temple. Enlil was not able to escape cosmic law, however, and because of his distortion of earth and spiritual forces, the tower was razed to the ground as soon as the Naphidem tried to descend.

In an unparalleled fury, Enlil let rip on Sumer. He had created a substance derived from gold in a process of reversed alchemy that could be used as a weapon of mass destruction, and this he turned on Sumer. It fell into molten ruins within minutes, allowing only a few of its people to escape, some of whom chronicled the terrifying event.

Enlil's Plan B now swung into action: a long, slow gathering of humanity into his lethal trap. He kept trying to revert to Plan A throughout history, in order to make a quick end of us, but his plans were thwarted each time by Enki and Nin-Khursag and their followers, among them, of course, the great beacons of spiritual teaching and mastery who have come to the rescue of humanity down the centuries. One of his last attempts to fast track his enterprise, and the greatest of all, consisted of the two world wars, the first of which culminated in the Nazi uprising in Germany. For the Nazis were inspired by, and were preparing for, the earthly invasion of the Naphidem.

We have left Nietzsche on the mountain top, or, more accurately, in the Upper Engadine valley, where, as he wrote, he awaited inspiration 'two thousand metres above good and evil'.

The following is what I think happened to Nietzsche on that fateful morning among the mountains.

Chapter Nine
THE MAGIC MIRROR

Nietzsche had been set a test in Wagner's opera house in Bayreuth, and had passed it with flying colours. He had rejected what was sent to corrupt him.

He was in preparation for what spiritual masters call the 'years of fire' which were encompassed by the two world wars. Enlil, by ingenious means, and particularly by manipulating the thought-sphere around the earth (much easier to imagine since the invention of the World Wide Web), had got into every religious system and every ideology on the planet. They each espoused aspects of the teachings of light, but there were within them all certain influences, sometimes surreptitious, sometimes brazen, which were designed to throw the human soul off course, so that there was no possibility of universal enlightenment. These seeds of nastiness in the small print arose from humanity's enchained vision. They were seeds that Enlil watered and fed, and in many cases purposely scattered.

The second of the untold stories may be set out in a few sentences. From the derivative of gold and other noble metals that Enlil had created by distorting the principles of alchemy – that pure spiritual knowledge of which Enki was initially in charge – Enlil was able to create not only weapons of mass destruction, but a food. It was called 'shew bread' in the Bible, and it consisted of a fragrant white powdery substance with a delicately sweet taste.

It was produced by perverting alchemical procedures so that, at the point during heating where gold and other high-degree metals become weightless and are caught up into a pure spiritual dimension, they instead enter a very different sphere – that of Enlil. Here, Enlil was able to scramble the integrity of the atoms of the metals and breathe certain malignant influences into these powerfully charged and dynamically creative receptacles that comprise the particles of gold.

When the treated metals returned to the earthly plane (for their journey was that of a circle upward into higher – or, when Enlil was involved, different – dimensions which ended where the circle began – at the point of inception on earth), there was in the crucible just a little mound of this fragrant white powder, consisting of very fine, soft particles, like a highly refined flour. Enlil's rendition of this powder (in contradistinction to the true alchemical version) carried with it the strange atonal music of spiritual misinformation: what Mary calls in her gospel 'guileful wisdom', which is displaced wisdom emanating from a seat other than the heart. It leads the soul away from spiritual truth and into a morass, although, in the manner of an alluring marsh light, it flickers like a tantalizing guide showing the safe path.

Enlil fed this substance to the kings and priests of the special bloodline that had been created to help humanity to reconnect itself. He thereby ensured that they would disseminate confusion and chaos to their people as well as the wisdom they drank from a divine source. This admixture of light and darkness could be relied upon to reduce the chance of any nation, culture or people on earth enabling itself to lead humanity to global enlightenment and so scuppering his cherished plan.

With his scientific colleague, Enlil found a way not only to dispense the white powder made according to his own special recipe as a physical substance, but also, by employing its ethereal counterpart whose pattern he had mastered, of feeding it at the etheric level as an invisible substance to people of power and influence who could afterwards be relied upon to help his cause. Of course, those who were thus targeted always had the option of refusing the influences carried into their perceptual centres via the sweet distorted gold. Yet, looking back on human history, it has to be said that few exercised their right to this option. Sadly, many good people fell into his clutches, seduced by the siren of power.

The 'years of fire' represented the infernal fires of the lower dragon which, because of the unrelenting stance of humanity in refusing true enlightenment and thereby stoking them up, were destined to be released upon the earth. They would comprise the Naphidem's greatest and most recent attempt to colonize the planet and in so doing, unwittingly play straight into the hands of Enlil. They would thus present humanity with the greatest struggle in its history, and yet simultaneously offer a release into true emancipation if the challenge were met.

According to Zarathustra, there were two great influences in the world, one good and one bad. These were equally matched in that they were twins or brothers. The good influence was Ahura Mazda, another name for the Sumerian Enki, as scholarship demonstrates. The evil brother was one whom Zarathustra called Ahriman. Again, scholarship proves, by many diverse routes, that Ahriman definitely equates with Enlil, or El-Elyon, he who had his seat of spiritual power at the meeting point of the two great rivers, the Euphrates and the Tigris.

Nietzsche's star was rising. He had come into his own light. His genius was of an order that set him apart as a potential luminary for the new age. For that very reason, the adversarial powers had cast their Cyclopian eye upon him and had targeted him, seeking to foster the seeds of weakness and 'unwisdom' in him. Yet he had overcome Enlil's attempt to call him into his service. He had resisted the anti-Semitism active in his own time, and deplored nationalism, though only because it militated against individualism.

It is worth mentioning here that it seems that the Jewish people were chosen by God to contain the terrible emanations and death-energies of Enlil in order to protect humanity from him. Their spiritual strength, which included a special grounding element, held him and his intentions in a powerful circle of damage limitation, although inevitably it cost them dire suffering. The descent from Cain produced Abraham, and it was this descent that carried forward the special bloodline, initiated for the purpose of providing a stairway down which certain evolved souls could travel once the great connection between heaven and earth had been cut off.

Realizing that Abraham and Sarah were the point of issue for a certain strengthening and redirection of this bloodline after it had borne its greatest fruit so far in Zarathustra or Ham, Enlil attached himself to them and called himself Jehovah: 'I Am That I Am.' He thought he could constantly hijack the influence of the true Jehovah (Mother–Father God) and cause Abraham and his issue to dance to his tune.

He believed that the Jewish nation was actively helping him to fulfil his plans. When he learned that they were protecting humanity from him, his ire was monumental and he began to form strategies to bring about the infamous 'Final Solution', for vengeful as well as strategic reasons.)

Having refused Enlil's call, Nietzsche was now ready for that historical moment when he would be offered the truth of Ahura Mazda, God of Light. This, of course, was Enki or (J)O(h)annes, the 'John' who was the 'one who came before' the Christ to prepare the way, just as John the Baptist did in the literal outplaying of this cosmic drama.

However, Nietzsche the Libran, the soul who at birth had inspired the momentous question from his father, 'Will he be good or will he be evil?', and who ever sought to transcend the duality of good and evil, could not escape his fate. It was written in the stars that, at the moment when an envoy of Ahura Mazda should approach him, an envoy of Ahriman should also draw commensurately near. He had won his moment with Zarathustra; but would he listen to him, or to his contester?

The final part of the second story can now be revealed. Enlil did not only create a weapon of mass destruction from reversed alchemy as well as a treacherous, perception altering food that could be taken both ethereally and physically. He also created a mirror of global dimensions, which was atomized and set invisibly in the heavens, or the atmosphere surrounding our planet. It encircled the planet in the form of a ring made from malignant gold.

This may sound too much like a feat from a Brothers Grimm story, and a few years ago such an observation could not have been denied. However, the US military have recently created something called 'smart dust'.

It is a weapon that consists of millions of particles as tiny as the scarcely visible components of dust, each one of which is an infinitesimal computer. These elfin 'computers' record co-ordinates and other information relating to the people and positions they settle upon, relaying this information to a central computer.

Whether in use (as has been claimed) or still in development, the existence of such dust seems to invest the idea of a global mirror floating atomized in the atmosphere with a modicum of probability. Like 'smart dust', its particles were reflective, for, although they were formed from alchemically treated gold and other noble metals, they differed from the white powder in that they consisted of glass. At a certain point during the heating and cooling mechanism used to create the white powder (both the true alchemical product and Enlil's rendition of it), it melted into liquid glass.

The Knights Templar, who created alchemically manufactured glass for their cathedrals, called it 'Spiritus Mundi', the 'spirit of the universe'. It was evoked into being by human breath, which was part of the alchemical process. Just prior to their transformation, the metals employed to make the (uncorrupted) white powder and, subsequently, the glass, would emit a glow of brilliant white light. It was this mystical light that the glass captured and reflected. The fact that it was referred to as Spiritus Mundi is most interesting, because although the term has esoteric implications, it is also true that the only method whereby gold and the other noble metals used in alchemy are forged in the universe is when a star is about to die. It bursts into an eruption of purest, brightest light, and it is only this final cataclysm of heat, much greater than any temperature it has reached throughout the span of its life, that is able to produce gold and the higher metals. Gold is the swansong of the stars.

However, in the case of Enlil's glass, the released light that the glass captured was of a very different nature. It was sinister and hypnotic. It was not a light of giving forth, of self-sacrifice, like the light from the stupendous fire-burst of a dying star, or the light emitted from gold before its atoms transform during the correct alchemical procedure. It was a light that sucked in: a vampiric, lurid light, and simultaneously a radiation that did psychic harm, like a burst of anger. It carried the power to distort perception, as did Enlil's version of the white powder, only in the case of the glass it was a continuous bombardment. One of its effects was to make important things look irrelevant, and unimportant things seem worthy of hugely intense and consistent focus.

I believe that Zarathustra appeared to Nietzsche to try to tell him of these things: that indeed the God of religion is a concept that cannot contain the highest aspirations and ideals of western civilization, because the way that religion has been receiving intimations of God is fundamentally flawed and purposely manipulated. It is imperative that we must now be freed from the restriction and burden of the limitations of our perception. History demands an entirely new ethical system, which is not built upon the big-otries and dogmas that undermine true faith, but reaches beyond the narrow concepts of a spiteful and self-satisfied morality that revels in judgementalism and is fired by the desire to condemn and punish. Our individual aspiration is indeed what, above all else, should fuel us. And our highest aspiration should certainly be to transcend ourselves, to lift ourselves onto the next rung of our personal evolution.

Nothing is more important than to strive to overcome our animal nature and thereby reach upward to attain the crown of that higher evolution, which is absorption into the super-human. We should, in fact, be fired by no other ideal than to become super-human ... or, as Mary expresses it in her gospel, 'fully' human. Thus spake Zarathustra.

I believe Zarathustra advocated Gnosticism, the spiritual discipline of inner knowing, which might translate loosely into 'individualism' because it teaches individual realization of God. He was, after all, the great inspiration of the Gnostics, who interpreted Christianity very differently from the Church of Rome and the Eastern Orthodox Church. And the great focal point of the Gnostics is the mystery of the mirror, as though they intuited Enlil's abuse and distortion of its divine qualities. They believed that the individual should find a direct route to God, and should not rely on any priesthood to act as intermediary. They understood the manipulation that was abroad, which sought to hijack their ascension to heaven while still on earth. The Gnostics were, in fact, seeking the ancient connection with God that everyone on earth had had the chance to enjoy before the striking of the Dolorous Blow, and which, of course, was exactly what Enki sought to teach.

These teachings, which culminated in the teachings of Christ, were perfected in the understanding of the Cathars, who arose at the turn of the first millennium in what is now southern France, but was in their day the land of Occitania, a country contiguous with but separate from France itself. It is easy to misunderstand their philosophy, because the version of it given out to the world seems nihilistic in many of its aspects. However, the understanding of the outer world was bound to remain skewed, because it did not have access to the inner sanctum of their vision.

It seems that even some of the initiated Cathars themselves could fall by the wayside in their efforts to hit the perceptual mark. There is every indication, in fact, that the beliefs of Schopenhauer which so seized Nietzsche with their nihilistic fervour arose from a source connected with Cathar beliefs that were thus off-kilter. Here, again, we see evidence of Enlil's withering breath influencing the flow of human thought into the channels in which he had an invested interest: those of ultimate hopelessness and death.

And yet the Cathars' true faith espouses a continuous bid for life in its most perfect and potent expression. Their aim was to eliminate from it all things that were breathed into it by the lower dragon of death and destruction and to liberate it into its full potential, a theme dealt with directly by Mary's gospel, and to which the teachings of Christ within that gospel give express focus. There within its wording, too, is the urge toward attaining our 'superhuman' selves or, much more accurately, our 'fully human' selves, because our humanity is not an animal, as Nietzsche had been led to believe, but divinity, calling us on to the highest heights. The esoteric insights of the Cathars were connected with the Sphere of John (Oannes or Enki), and their rites were deeply powerful, enshrining secrets that, because of orthodoxy, were not made known to the world. They were rites that Enki had taught them. The most profound and mystical of them all was the *Consolamentum*. It contained the deepest and most potent of the secrets of the Cathars, which was a part of the power of the previous connection itself.

Leonardo de Vinci knew of this secret and was almost

certainly a Cathar. His painting of the Last Supper spells out, in reverse, the word *Consolamentum*. The letters equate with the line of disciples, each of whom bears a name in Latin assigned to them by Jacobus de Voraigne in his work *The Golden Legend,* where he gave an account of their lives. The names were descriptive of their qualities, and it is the first letter of each of these Latin names, with Christ in their midst denoted as 'Alpha', that reveals the word '*Consolamentum*'. The *Consolamentum* was associated with the Holy Grail, and was said to contain a part of its secrets. The third story in our sequence that waits to be told will concern the mystery of the Grail.

Zarathustra came to Nietzsche with his gift of light, bearing elements of the Grail. He shone with the radiance of the sacred dragon, the Pendragon. He sought to reveal the secret of the ages in imparting to Nietzsche how humanity had been controlled for so long by a god of wrath and vengeance and cruel morality – a god who was not a god at all, and ought to be denounced for what he was – an imposter. He sought to reveal how vital it was for us all to escape his clutches and to rise into our true humanity, which was indeed a superlative state compared to the imprisoned, helpless, blinded, branded and crawling creatures we had been reduced to. He sought to reveal how our route to God involved the veneration of the Sacred Feminine, our own source of wisdom, our intuition.

He gave Nietzsche a vision, glorious to behold, of what we could become, of what life on earth would transfigure into, once we had passed through the Divine Forges of the higher fires of the Pendragon.

Zarathustra urged him to see the dualism in life from an inspired perspective. It was exemplified by the human influences of Enki and Enlil, the good and the evil brothers, on earthly civilizations. The mighty spirits of light and darkness that stood behind them were woven into the tapestry of creation and were as two great interconnecting wheels of life, one above, one below.

Yet the dynamics of this great unified wheel need not throw us into outer darkness. It is only when we move towards what is evil that the dark wheel actually produces and releases evil, and consequently throws everything off balance. It is human choice that works the magic, for good or for ill. All we have to do to find the point of balance is to move always toward the good, towards the light. Then dualism will be transcended and all will work together for good. From the mountain tops of life, from our transcendental point above the conjoined wheels of light and darkness, we would see that their interconnectedness exists in order to create greater good, brighter light, deeper penetration of Divine possibility.

Zarathustra set Nietzsche the great task of stepping through the mirror, and thus shattering the false reflection that Enlil had created for millennia. All the interior resources he needed were there to support him, although he would have to struggle mightily with the dark and ignorant elements within him to make the breakthrough into truth and freedom.

But by Zarathustra's side, seeking to obliterate his light, stood Marduk.

Chapter Ten
THE EVIL TWIN

Marduk pushed his way forward again and again. He sought to superimpose himself over Zarathustra. Nothing could be done, because it was entirely dependent on Nietzsche's free choice as to whom he gave ear to. Marduk's voice became more and more insistent. Eventually, it seemed to take on the essence and characteristics of Zarathustra's voice. This time, something within Nietzsche did not cast him out. He found a foothold. Nietzsche listened.

Rudolf Steiner, the great thinker and teacher of spiritual truth, tells us that the principle of evil is a split principle. He was a man who saw with Zarathustra's vision, and he warned us that Satan is always accompanied by Lucifer. These two fundamental spirits of evil hate one another with a raging and poisonous hatred, yet they always work together in tandem like conjoined twins.

Satan is the dark, dreary, sinister, calculating, life-sucking force that imprisons, restricts, obstructs, imposes suffering through indifference and chills the marrow. He works through the principle of ice. He wants to bind us to the earth and to see us perish in the brittle and unrelentingly limiting shell of materialism. He wants to maintain an absolute impenetrability within the structure of that shell. He drags down and enchains.

He loves machines and would teach us that we and the

whole of the cosmos are one great insentient machine, grinding out life without purpose or divine inspiration.

He rules us by fear and doubt. His cold, hard reasoning will say, 'Let's be realistic', in a move to wither any inspiration or positive gesture as it buds from the heart. He exacts a price and imposes punishment. He is 'the slayer of the real'.

Enlil expresses this stance. In Nietzsche's terms, the culprit was Apollo, the god of the sun who cast the hard, unforgiving daylight into the most cherished and secret places of the soul, and whose calculating logic and reason destroyed the magic of life. This understanding does not equate very well with the spirit of darkness, and yet we might call what Enlil represents an aspect of the false light: the dark component of the false light that destroys, blinds and casts the real and the true into exile and invisibility. Of course, this is exactly what Enlil does, while masquerading as the one true God of ineffable light. His mirror reflects a false light and serves his cause to perfection.

Lucifer is the fiery principle of evil. Here we see the incendiary nature of the lower dragon come into its own. Lucifer stokes up the human ego and encourages us to think only of ourselves and our own desires. He can hardly bear to be upon the earth. He wants us to rise into a sense of our own self-importance and grandeur. He is the wielder of self-will and self-glorification. He wants the individual ego to claim absolute power and declare itself as all-powerful. He inflicts pain for the joy of it. Tyranny, dictatorship, crushing others under the heel, are his great ideals. Madness and disintegration are his gifts. 'Do what thou wilt shall be all the law,' says Lucifer. He is glamorous and seductive, rather than chilling and terrifying, although, of course, once seduction has occurred, he is very terrifying indeed!

Both of these great lords of evil are masters of the Lie. They constantly tell lies to humanity about our intrinsic selves and about the nature of reality.

It can be seen that Enlil was Satan's puppet, and Marduk was Lucifer's. Nietzsche had successfully countered Enlil's approaches, but he fell straight into Marduk's clutches, although not wholly, because Zarathustra is there in Nietzsche's expositions as well as Marduk, the evil twin of Zarathustra's light. This would seem to fit the pattern, because, just as the dark Enlil twinned the bright Enki, so Marduk, the false light, twinned Zarathustra, the true light. There is even a historical pairing between these two, as there was between the royal brothers Enki and Enlil, because Marduk was of the dreaded Naphidem and was fathered by Enki, while Ham, or Zarathustra, bore within him the genetic inheritance of Enki's sperm from Cain, and was Enki's (seven times) great-grandson.

And, strangely and yet so aptly, at the turn of the last century, the countdown to the 'years of fire', German archaeologists unearthed Babylon, the city over which Marduk was given control as a god by Anu and Enlil, and, with the approval of the Ottoman authorities, transported all its relics to Berlin, so soon to be the capital of the Third Reich. They reconstructed some of its main features there, where it can still be visited today. As far as the history of the Reich is concerned, Marduk had come home.

It is chilling to think that this happened less than a generation after Nietzsche had written his great work *Thus Spake Zarathustra*. Everything was moving into place on the world stage. Marduk had set up his camp in waiting, and he must have glorified in the contemplation of the thousand-year Reich that he thought was coming.

The removal of Babylon to Berlin was undeniably synchronicitous, because a contemporaneous description of the German mind-set in the years leading up to World War I cited it as being 'fervent, warlike, and full of Nietzsche' (*Concise Universal Biography*, London, 1930). Adolf Hitler, of course, was waiting in the wings, clasping *Thus Spoke Zarathustra* to his eager heart as he endured the trench warfare of the Great War.

Zarathustras's truth, nevertheless, does shine through in many of Nietzsche's insights. He concluded, for instance, in *The Birth of Tragedy*, published in 1872, that the original genius of Greece, and the proper state of humankind, was an instinctive and joyous creativeness that he designated the 'Dionysiac element', which was ruined by the material positivism and the rigid moral attitudes of the 'Apollinist element'. This stance was developed further in his great work, and of course is music to the ears of those of us who long to transcend the dull, heavy stultification of the mundane world.

But the Nazi ideology, the contempt for the weak and helpless, the glorification of war and of the individual over the common good, the railing against democracy, all are ever-present in his doctrines, which are profoundly Luciferian. Just as, inconceivably long ago, Enlil and Anu had plotted that Marduk should strike the Dolorous Blow against Mother God, not only destroying our direct connection with heaven, but also shattering the power of the Sacred Feminine in our world, now Nietzsche, in microcosm, did the same. His location for this deed was the Alpine village of Saint Mary, situated in a valley, symbol of Divine Mother. That was where he raised the intrinsic sword, and brought it down with an executioner's zeal.

He advocated the masculine 'Will to Power' as the only true value in existence, and proclaimed that men were at their finest when they knew no law other than their own individual self-will. The values and qualities of the Sacred Feminine he absolutely castigated. With eerie prophecy, which, thank goodness, was prevented from realization by the Allied Forces, he believed that there would one day arise a society of 'Over-Men' who would 'transvaluate values' and create a 'master morality' of their own. He foresaw the coming of the Naphidem. Later, leaving him in violent fits of quaking dread in which blood streamed from inside his ears – episodes that are described in official and verified contemporary documents – Hitler met with their terrible leader, shrieking, 'He is here! He is here! The New Man is here!'

The 'New Man' was in fact Marduk's great mission. The clay tablets from ancient Sumer record the history of how, many thousands of years ago, Marduk, Enlil and Anu all tried to formulate the 'New Man' on earth, via biological experimentation in the manner of the Nazis, but failed. It was, it seems, an ancient record of yet another attempt to re-establish the Naphidem on earth.

Another term from these times was 'the New World Order', again documented in just such exact terms on the ancient clay tablets. This was a plan that Mother God had for the earth and all her peoples, to be put into implementation by Enki and Nin-Khursag. Enlil, with his sinister motives, took over this plan, and sought to supplant it with his own New World Order, the horrible culmination of which he wishes to see actualized in our own time.

However, if we all play our part, no matter how humble it may seem, we are assured of victory over this dark and savage New World Order, Enlil-style, and will instead see the true New World Order rise up with healing in its wings for all humanity.

What Nietzsche advocated is, of course, pure Naphidem philosophy; and Nietzsche certainly helped to promote the unfolding of Armageddon in the twentieth century. Racked with illness, suffering prohibitive weakness of body, and, after a devastating seizure, descending into an insanity from which he never recovered, the question arises: what might a ruthless and cruel society of 'Over-Men' have done with him.

Many positive influences have arisen from Nietzsche's power to inspire, and from some of his ideas. Great evil also strengthened its grip on the world via the conduit of his writings. He seconded the Dolorous Blow, and yet to some degree he also served divine truth. He expressed Zoroastrian dualism to perfection, and therefore his quest ultimately failed. Whatever his claims, he did not rise above good and evil, but emanated both, with the emphasis perhaps firmly on the dark side.

Nietzsche's story serves as a tutelary one of the greatest importance as we contemplate working with the Ka angels. We are approaching another watershed in human history. It is vital that, this time, we get it right.

The Ka angels are here to help us to transcend ourselves, to fire us with the notion that we can become 'superhuman' or fully human. They will open up to us the vista of the stars. We just have to be careful that, in rushing to greet them, we do not hurtle headlong into the abyss.

Chapter Eleven
MITHRA, ANGEL OF GLORY

There is a secret to be revealed regarding Mithra, the 'glorious angel', known as the mystic son of Michael and Shekinah. The rites of Mithra were mysterious and hidden. Above all others, Mithra, 'the unconquerable sun', was the angel that Zarathustra most praised and held in greatest awe. Nothing has come down to us from anecdotal history or from any kind of textual record regarding the ceremonies of Mithra. There are statements regarding his extraordinary power, beauty and radiance. There are statements praising his divine eminence and grandeur. There are statements warning about the foolhardiness of misusing Mithraic influence or appearing before him without a scrupulously pure heart. Everything else is lost forever, and perhaps never even existed in material form. Zoroastrian Mithraic initiates kept profoundly solemn vows of silence that extended to ciphers as well as to the spoken word.

Mithra is definitely a Ka angel and, in a sense, the most important of all. Michael and Shekinah stand at the pinnacle of the angelic hierarchy, and yet could not work with humanity as they do without Mithra. It can be said that Mithra is an aspect of them, but he–she is so intimately linked to them, and there is such an interchange of creative communion between them, that it is as if Mithra is their child.

Mithra is the point of connection between heaven and earth, and constitutes a shining Jacob's ladder that bridges the dimensions. Mithra is therefore associated with the heavenly connection to earth that humanity enjoyed prior to the striking of the Dolorous Blow.

I have been given a number of simple rites that can be used to help those who seek to connect with Mithra as a Ka angel. Some of his mysteries will be revealed with the presentation of these rites. We will revisit the scenario whereby a star in its dying burst forges gold. Mithra will teach us the sacrificial aspect to the formation of gold, and he will teach us secrets about the magic mirror and the golden twin.

First, we must make a clear distinction between Mithra, the angel of glory, and Mithras, the Roman god of glory in battle. There are many pointers to indicate that the two are interlinked, and that Mithras arose from the Zoroastrian concept of Mithra. Again, the Roman Mithraic rites were very closely guarded. No evidence anywhere suggests that Mithra and Mithras shared the same identity. However, there is reason to believe that in some respects, the rites of Mithras were the degenerate rites of Mithra.

An icon commonly unearthed at Mithraic sites is one which appears to have represented the terrible lion-headed goddess of the Egyptian pantheon who is clearly referenced in Egyptian and Babylonian myth as joining Enlil's party of conspirators when he plotted to kill humanity. Because of the terrible outrages of the Naphidem, this goddess vowed to help Enlil to 'drown the human world in a great tide of its own blood'.

She would do this, she vowed, by keeping humankind perpetually at war with one another. Several dedications to Deus Arimanius – Ahriman or Enlil – have come to light, one of them on a headless statue in York, England, which is considered to be a depiction of this same lion-headed deity.

Rumours of the era tell of a secret sect of the priests of Mithras, which practised horrific rites dedicated to the lion-headed or cat goddess. The rites involved unspeakably obscene and barbaric sacrifices of foetuses, babies, children and animals. In the novel *The Angel of the West Window* by the Austrian writer Gustav Meyrink, the author suggests that these rites developed into the cult of the Thracian 'Black Isäis', a perversion of the true Isis who was a reflection of the boundless beauty and goodness of Mother God.

Although it is a fictional account, there is no doubt that Meyrink's 'Isäis' was synonymous with the same blood-thirsty lion-headed goddess whose declared aim was to cause hatred and war among humanity until it finally annihilated itself. Her tentacles, like Enlil's, extended all over the world. In Britain, the vile *Taghairm* rites took root, which summoned the cat goddess by putting to death a large number of cats in an act of highly ritualized and diabolical cruelty too disgusting to relate.

The Celtic peoples, linked by ancestry to the ancient Egyptians where the first conception of the dark Mithraic rites arose, sacrificed oxen and spilt blood from their sacrifice on the land. In his disturbing epic poem, 'Gaudete', Ted Hughes tells of an elemental spirit, arising from the powers of mass bloodshed and lust-centred sexual rites, who in human form wanders the west of Ireland composing hymns and psalms to an obscure female deity.

The two books even share a character: 'Gartner' in the first and 'Garten' in the second, who relate to the spiritual 'gardener' of the earth and of the soul. The divinely inspired 'Gardener' ensures that the malignancies of Mammon are challenged and that the earth and the human soul continue to enjoy the ability to express paradise and to cherish the seeds of paradise within their combined heart.

In such works of imaginative vision we can catch glimpses of the reality of the reversed goddess, the false mirror image of the true originating Goddess of All. Her glory was reviled and her memory was overlaid by the hideous Dark Mother whose power was that of the biblical entity 'Mammon', the spirit of materialism and imprisoning materiality, which was concerned with scuppering the true rites of the Zoroastrian Mithra and ensuring that humanity remained unable to achieve ascension and receive the divine and inconceivable blessing of the Holy Grail.

This goddess of cruelty, sexual perversion and brutality is not to be confused with the Black Madonna, who has an entirely opposite, positive and beautiful symbolism, in that her light is of such ineffable grandeur and brightness that it appears to our attenuated vision as blackness; nor to the Egyptian Basht, who was a kindly goddess of happiness and well-being. To the ancient Egyptians, cats were venerable even above other sacred animals, and to harm or kill one, even accidentally, was considered a crime punishable by death.

According to Meyrink, the priests of Mithras who developed the cult of the lion-headed goddess were profound in their worship of the adversarial forces.

After causing the evil goddess to manifest in their vision by enactment of their brutal and monstrous rites, they proceeded to dress in women's clothing and approach her with the left side of their bodies (the feminine orientation according to arcane law). They then offered her their adoration, proven by their sacrifice to her of their perception and sense of their own maleness. Some, in their frenzy, even made a ritual physical amputation of their manhood.

This distressing act was not encouraged, because the point of the cult and its rites was to engender hatred and strife between the sexes rather than to create eunuchs. The true balance and interchange on many subtle levels between a man and a woman, which is expressed in the rites of the Sacred Marriage, is the power that halts war and human outrage. The rites of the cat goddess were created as an attempt to entirely unhinge the possibility of the healing of the Sacred Marriage occurring on a worldwide scale.

They comprised the converse side of the all-male cult of Mithras, with its cruel sacrifice of bulls and its sole emphasis on masculinity and war, and did not involve men getting in touch with their feminine side, with which transvestites are associated today.

Although nothing extant proves the ancient rumours and Meyrink's interpretation of them in his symbolic story, he was an occult writer who belonged to several mystic brotherhoods whose archives and artefacts were never in the public domain. There are many indicators to suggest that his imaginative insights may align with ancient actuality.

Sacrifice to the evil Ahrimanic forces was certainly practised by adherents of the blatant satanic religions of the time. These do not include the religion of the worship of Mithras, as it encompassed a higher purpose as well as degenerate rites.

Its adherents generally did not know about the secret Mithraic priesthood and the poison that exuded from its clandestine ceremonies. It is interesting that wolves were the designated sacrificial animals for the rites of the openly satanic religions, because the wolf links Ahriman with

Mithras and Rome. Mithras was the championed deity of the Roman military, who evidentially might have worshipped him via Ahrimanically-distorted rites to Mithra; and Rome was conceived and built by Romulus and Remus, the twin brothers who were famously suckled by a wolf.

The custom of sacrificing animals in religious ceremonies, and particularly of slaying the sacred bull, arose from the influences of Enlil. It was, as usual, a crudely and unnecessarily literalized rendition of a sacred inner truth – a favourite trick of his.

He was well aware that spiritual law decrees there will be bloodshed upon the earth between men while ever animals are slain by human hands, and he took particular pains to encourage the practice, sowing seeds of repulsion against vegetarianism, so that it became known as 'the Devil's Banquet'. Those who partook of it were branded as sinister, unsavoury and sinning against the will of God: a bigotry that has persisted until the present day.

In fact, we can find an illustration of Enlil's stance among the very first stories of the Bible: the history of Cain and Abel. Earlier sources than the books of the Old Testament confirm that Cain, the son of Enki and Eve and the first product of the special bloodline, was the foremost priest of the Temple of Enki, while Abel was Enlil's high priest. Abel was Eve's son by Adam, her earthly husband. He was easily manipulated and a much less inspired soul than Cain, his brother.

The Bible tells us that God was pleased with the sacrificial offerings of Abel, who brought him 'the firstlings of his flock and the fat thereof', but was not pleased with the offerings of Cain, on whose sacrificial altars there was no sizzling and melting of fat and flesh, but only offerings of fruit and grain. In fact, this story represented Enlil's attempt at a takeover of Enki's temple, for it was Enki who had taught his followers to sacrifice only fruit, grain and honey to Mother–Father God as a symbolic offering of the soul, and never to harm or kill animals for human benefit.

Enlil, on the other hand, already an egomaniac, accepted offerings made in his temple for himself, and insisted that they were animal sacrifices. However, there was method in his madness, as he knew only too well the negative effects on the human soul of killing its animal brethren. There followed an attempted coup, in which Abel died at the hands of the royal guard while trying to murder Cain, upon which Cain was unfairly banished from the land. Bands of vigilantes who had supported Abel were incited to seek him out and kill him, but Enki guarded him with angelic and spiritual protection, which was summoned by the symbol of the 'Mark of Cain'. This was a cross of light within a ring of light which could be seen shining out from Cain's forehead at the point of the 'unicorn's horn' chakra (at the top of the forehead in the middle), keeping potential evil-doers at bay. (Chakras are points in the body where the physical and spiritual forces interface.)

According to ancient texts comprising the Talmud and the Old Testament, Lilith, rather than Eve, Cain's mother, was Adam's 'first wife', who refused his sexual advances and deserted him. She is spoken of as an evil spirit. Earlier Sumerian sources, on which the stories of the Old Testament are based, state that Lilith was, in fact, Enki's second wife, and that Nin-Khursag, Lilith and Enki came together as a unit committed to the project of spiritual and genetic engineering that would enable humanity to achieve the heights of perceptual development. They did this in secrecy and in the face of great danger, because Enlil would have killed them all if he had suspected the truth. They were obeying the injunctions of Mother God, and were prepared to risk everything in order to do so. Enki was cited as the 'snake' in the Garden of Eden, the one who followed the guidance of the 'serpent', Tiâmat (Mother God, or the Dragon Queen). Enki was the 'Evil One' – according to Enlil. Earlier sources definitely link the Hebraic Samael, equated with the snake of Eden, with the Sumerian Enki. It is a point on which scholars concur.

Nin-Khursag, Enki's first wife, gave physical birth to both Adam and Eve (interestingly, Eve came first rather than Adam) via artificial insemination. Enki's sperm was used for the conception of both babies, whilst ova were donated by two earthly mothers. Eve was nursed by Nin-Khursag, while Adam's nurse was Lilith. Eve and Adam were a designated couple from the start, intended for one another as husband and wife. However, as soon as Eve came of age, it was her destiny to bear Enki's son, Cain. A wife of similar high spiritual status, Luluwa, was brought into being for Cain, using the same method of insemination via Lilith. However, meanwhile, because of Eve's special relationship with Enki, Adam became jealous and began to insist on sexual relations with Lilith, his warden and instructress, as compensation for his wife's interest in Enki. Lilith refused him and, ultimately, persuaded him to accept Eve's carnal relations with Enki, because it was explained to him that the earthly human/higher Anunnaki initiated bloodline had to descend through the earthly matriarchal line. Adam was finally reconciled to this, but not Abel, who hated Cain because he had a different father, and because Cain was the one chosen to inherit Adam's priest-kingship (priest of the Temple of Enki). This was why Abel switched sides and went over to Enlil, who was quick to promise him succession – if he would kill Cain first to get him out of the way!

The cult of Mithras was not by any means wholly 'evil', of course. It is not within Enlil's power to make humankind completely subservient to the principle of evil, however hard he tries.

The worshippers of Mithras learned many noble things, among them the virtues of honour and bravery, the loyalty due to friendship, the importance of following through, keeping promises and meeting contractual obligations. Yet women were strictly prohibited from participating in the religion, and it served the masculine principle to an unbalanced degree. It appears to have become a soldiers' cult, designed to inspire warriors in the field, not only as defenders but as pillagers, sackers and marauders. Unconquerability and invincibility in warfare and the consequent Luciferian pumping up of the ego seem to have been its main focus. And there were within it sinister, satanic rites, which turned away decisively from 'the Unconquered Sun'.

These rites cherished the horror of the Minotaur in their heart, and their invocants worshipped this monstrous slayer of men and, significantly, devourer of women, who were specifically and ritualistically sacrificed to the creature. Intimations of Nietzsche come to mind, where he rails against women and their dangerous propensity to value the principle of love above all things. 'You go to women? Take a whip,' he advises endearingly.

Despite the religion's loftier precepts, Enlil won the day with his corruption of Mithra into Mithras. Strife, hatred and bloodletting held sway across the earth as the centuries passed. All the undeniable dynamism and richness of human history came into manifestation, but ignoble and squalid influences, ever-present and seemingly ineradicable, always prevented humanity from truly turning the corner and heading into its 'fully human' heritage.

Both Mithras and Mithra were the essence of 'the Unconquerable Sun', but in the case of Mithras, this essence of might and glory was to some degree fed into the ego. The pure Mithraic rites of Zoroaster are the only ones it is safe and sane to enter into. They involve a sacrifice of self rather than the knifing to death of some hapless bull so that human beings might capitalize on the potency of the spilling of its blood and the power of its death in sacrifice.

Bearing this in mind, let us turn decisively to the true Mithra, angel of the highest glory. For Mithra bears the secret of the Grail.

Chapter Twelve

THE SECRET OF THE HOLY GRAIL

To understand how Mithra is the Angel of the Holy Grail, we need to place Zarathustra in his ancestral context. His greatest (literal) ancestor was, of course, Enki, or Ahura Mazda, the god of light himself. Enki fathered Cain via the biblical Eve, but Eve herself, by special arrangement, had been born to Nin-Khursag, Enki's revered consort, and carried a particular inheritance in her DNA that Adam did not share.

The name 'Cain' is titular and is a contracted form of 'quayin'. It derives from 'ayin', the all-seeing eye which is a symbol for omniscience, fronted by 'Q', the feminine symbol, associated with both the moon and Venus and ultimately with the supreme Mother God. In another form it becomes the word 'queen', and is also the reference in ancient alchemy for a master smith or artificer. In all the dimensions of its mystery, Cain is a distinguished title indeed, for it denotes the master artificer or alchemist in service to the supreme queen of divine knowledge, or Mother God.

If we take nature as a guide, we see that, although alpha males rule many animal kingdoms, it is the insect queen-ships that are by far the most mysterious, awe-inspiring and powerful communities. They tend to occur in the insect domain because the human thought-sphere influences it less, or at least in a different and less direct way than the influence it casts over animal behaviour; for it is true, according to spiritual teaching, that animals, both wild and domestic, take their cue from the dominant traits that express themselves throughout the impulses and tendencies informing the energy of human thought. Enlil might have led the destructive movement that caused the wholesale denial of the Sacred Feminine, but he could not disrupt the alchemy of the insect queenships.

Cain inherited his title from his father Enki and continued Enki's mission on earth as his father's ambassador. Indeed, Enki was the appointed one, chosen by Mother God, first to fulfil her mission of establishing humanity on earth and forging it so that its soul reflected the divine image, and, after the horror of the Dolorous Blow, to continue to protect and educate it, to keep the divine light alive in human hearts, to foster the incarnation of spiritual teachers, and to guard the secret knowledge that was denied and banished by Enlil.

Laurence Gardner tells us that Cain is often referred to among esoteric circles as 'the first Mr Smith', because of his association with forging, smithship, alchemy and fire. This idea of celestial fire – the dragon principle – which creates, sustains and forges life and is the expression of divine light whose essence is our own, is also invariably associated with Zarathustra or Ham. Zarathustra did not teach the worship of fire, but of that spark of ineffable light which dwells within the heart and is the flame of our divinity. It is our direct connection to God, the source of all light, and it reveals that we are beings of light, born of the sacred dragon principle that will one day irradiate every atom of which we consist, and of which the planet consists, so that we are no longer physical and mundane, but caught up into the heart of God.

We will retain our individuality and our humanity, but we will be 'fully human'. We will be Pendragons, golden, of the essence of light, sun-like and crowned with the consciousness of God's ineffable fire.

Scientists now believe that, even at the mundane level, light equates with evolution on earth. A mountain range in Canada that preserves the world's oldest fossils shows a small worm or serpent-like creature, *Picaiah* (note the 'dragon' link), over half a billion years old, which is in the unprecedented process of developing an eye. Once the sacred 'ayin' had been evolutionally constructed, earthly life and consciousness could progress to their highest pinnacle: humanity. *Picaiah* is our earliest bodily forebear.

Zarathustra's inheritance from the Dragon Queen is indicated by his name and that of his illustrious ancestors. Eusebius, the Father of Church history, writing in the first century, tells us that the Zoroastrians named their concept of heaven or celestial paradise after the serpent: a secret acknowledgement that they were adorers of the Dragon Queen.

'Zarathustra' itself means 'golden dawn' or 'golden light', deriving from the word 'zara' (golden) and the word 'ushers' (light or dawn). (A linguistic Bahuvrihi compound deriving from the Avestan tongue gives us 'zarata', meaning 'old' and 'feeble', and 'usatra', meaning 'camels', translating to 'he who has old camels' or 'the feeble one who has old camels'. Scholarship gives us a choice, and since Zarathustra did indeed represent a new and golden dawn in the teachings of the light, I prefer the first. Nevertheless, glory couched in humility and poverty is typically how spirituality reveals itself.) My personal belief is that somehow 'Thoth', slightly altered because of localized linguistics and in fact allied to the English word 'truth' in the rabbit language, was a component of his name. Thoth represents the ancient Egyptian understanding of Enki and his secret temple. Zarathustra's name would therefore spell out 'zara' (golden) 'thust' (Thoth) 'ra' (light), meaning the 'the golden light of Thoth'.

Ham/Zarathustra was, in his mundane descent, firmly linked familially with the Egyptian strain. Nimrod the Mighty, a great king of Mesopotamia, was Ham's grandson, and Nimrod was the father of King Anedjib, the pharaoh of the first Egyptian dynasty, which came into being around 3000 BC. So Ham was the great-grandfather of the king who founded the Egyptian dynasties, and carried the seeds of the monumental Egyptian culture within him. His teachings were revered within it, although Enlil also had a foothold therein, and consequently there was a dark side to Egypt. (It was especially to the Egyptian kings, for instance, that Enlil fed his distorted gold as communion bread or *Schefa*-cakes, as they were known in ancient Egypt. They were little conical 'bread' cakes made from the corrupted white powder.) The notion that the name Zarathustra may carry Egyptian influences in its etymology is therefore a possibility.

There is no mistaking the names of his ancestors, however. Cain's actual name (Cain being a title) was Ar-wi-um. Its meaning is related to its Hebrew rendition, *awwim*, which translates as 'serpents'. One of Enki's alternative names was Masda or Mas-en-da, meaning 'one who prostrates himself as a serpent'. Many sources speak of a 'golden serpent' that is identifiable with Enki (see above). As the Persian tradition replaced the Sumerian, Enki became known as Ahura

Mazda, which contracted into Ormuzd, meaning 'Serpent of the Night'. This last name is echoed in Zarathustra's full name, Khem (sometimes Ham) or Chem-Zarathustra, because of the link with Khem and the night, or what simultaneously is hidden and yet revealed, as the night sky reveals the stars.

Khem has many mysterious and beautiful meanings. From one point of view, it became 'ken', the ken of Celtic 'knowing', indicating, in particular, sacred knowledge revealed by the intuition (the 'inner tutor'), and was related to the word 'Cain' or 'quayin'. From another aspect, it means 'darkness', but darkness of a sanctified nature, the good and positive component of what is known as the 'shining darkness', the darkness of the night, which so exquisitely reveals the stars.

From yet another observation point, it becomes a phrase meaning 'overcoming the darkness'. The darkness referred to is still the positive, restful darkness of creative silence, but the quest vouchsafed to the pupil by the darkness is to find the light shining deep within its bosom, which darkness itself makes possible. (Without darkness present in the frames of a film, for instance, our experience of it would simply be as a continuous beam of blinding light until it ended. We would not be able to distinguish any images whatsoever.)

From this concept the word pupil itself sprang, simultaneously meaning a student and the dark aperture in the eye that lets in the light. It is the duty of the 'pupil' to strive to 'comprehend' the light. This last endeavour is a little different from observing the revelation of the stars in that, in the first instance, the darkness itself reveals the light as a grace and a gift, whereas in the second instance, the pupil has to exert every strength within the soul, and translate potential strength latent there into fully flourishing potency, before the light is revealed. It is a process of initiation, and it leads back to Cain and the 'ayin', the single divine eye of revelatory consciousness, of exalted knowledge.

It is worth remembering that the scientific view supports the idea that, although the universe is currently expanding, it will one day contract and return to its initial form prior to the Big Bang: a tiny black point smaller than a grain of sand – the pupil of the 'ayin'.

So Chem-Zarathustra was 'Zarathustra the Quayin', just as Ar-wi-um (Cain) was 'Ar-wi-um the Quayin'. The bloodline had struck gold. Zarathustra had arrived. And, whether or not he was feeble and kept old camels, he was certainly the bringer of the golden dawn, the bringer of the light of heaven, the mouthpiece of the golden serpent.

There is one final meaning of the mystery of Chem. We have seen that it is to do with the sacred alchemy of overcoming the darkness and summoning the totality of the pupil's spiritual strength in order to perceive the deepest, brightest star hidden in the bosom of the night, and thus to be filled with the starlight of celestial knowledge. Once this was achieved, the initiate was said to receive the 'star fire', the secret essence of the Mother or the Dragon Queen, which was exalted consciousness. The pupil became the Pendragon, being now 'fully human'.

The central point about the star fire is this. It was spiritual apperception, but certain aspects of its application required education, the kind of understanding we achieve through instruction from a teacher. The teacher was our higher self, the part of us that resides in heaven. And because the connection between heaven and earth has been cut off via the

Dolorous Blow, there are some components of the divine knowledge that we can only receive, as if from a teacher, when we become a unified field of energy; that energy being humanity itself.

In other words, while we can receive the baptism of divine knowledge at an individual and personal level, and be exalted and transfigured by it, there are some elements to this divine knowledge that we cannot be given until we are ready as a global community to receive it together. We need to become as one merged Grail Cup of receptivity. So the Chem is a state of exalted consciousness, but it encompasses the consciousness of the whole as well as the individual.

In esoteric law, the Chem is represented as a pyramid-shaped emerald which occurs in masculine mode as the third eye, the seat of consciousness, and in feminine mode at the point of the uterus, the seat of the Dragon Queen, symbolizing the magic cauldron of consciousness from which higher perception arises.

The Emerald Tablet

It is time to consider the Emerald Tablet. Many tales are told of the wonder and the mystery of the Emerald Stone or Tablet. One myth relates that it was supposed to have fallen to the earth from Lucifer's crown at the point when he stumbled in his celestial heights and became corrupt. Ancient Sumerian sources tell us that it was originally the Table of Destiny of the Serpent People. This is the same precious repository as the Emerald Table of Thoth-Hermes and, as the alchemical records of Egypt make clear, the preserved records within it were written by the biblical Ham.

As we know, 'Ham' is a rendition of the Egyptian 'Hermes' (although the word itself is Greek). Thoth-Hermes was

Ham or Zarathustra giving forth the teachings of Enki, or Hermes giving forth the teachings of Thoth, for the teachers and the teachings are identical. Thoth was sometimes referred to in Egypt, for instance, as 'Father John', in recognition of his Oannes or Johannes status.

Hermes or Ham is associated with the art of pyramid construction as mentioned earlier, (*herma*, from which Hermes derives, is a reference to a certain or special 'pile of stones'). Ham instructed the Egyptians in building the pyramids, based on the old ziggurat form originating in Sumer, which was a pyramidal structure with steps leading to a temple at the pinnacle. Both edifices were magical, because both were associated with esoteric knowledge from the Emerald Tablet. Ham, as always, was guided and inspired by his spiritual father (and literal, many times removed, grandfather) Enki, or, in Egyptian cosmology, Thoth. The Great Pyramid was sometimes referred to as 'the Sanctuary of Thoth'.

The guarded secret of the pyramids is that they contain something, albeit severely restricted, of the magic of the former connection with God before the Dolorous Blow fell. The connection with God was the Grail itself ('such a holy thing' wrote Tennyson of it in his masterful poem, 'The Holy Grail'). It is helpful to understand it in the following way.

What we once could access because of our planetary connection to God was taken away from us. To make sure that this unspeakably vital and precious knowledge could not be lost to us forever (which was Enlil's great hope and plan), Mother God put it into a form of 'holding station' and gave it into Enki's care.

This holding station was a physical emerald of such a high and potent degree of perfection, its molecular complexity so exquisitely organized and its sub-atomic particles so beautifully ordered and so clarifyingly magnified to the loftiest gradation of purity, that it could absorb, as a gift of light taken into its heart, all the knowledge, all the divine information, that God had once made known to the earth and earth's humanity through the holy connection to God's heart that we had formerly enjoyed.

Why was it an emerald? The reason was simply because emerald green is the colour at the heart of the seven rays of creation, symbolized by the rainbow. It secretes the magic of the heart. And it was this power, the secret knowledge of the heart, which Enlil had wished to destroy and to supplant solely with the power of the mind and the power of the will.

He could not ultimately do it, of course. There was always the individual, personal way open to human beings so that, through much struggle and endeavour, they could properly realize God. Yet the grand, universal connection had been destroyed (again, not quite, but generally so). We can understand the Grail, therefore, as that prior connection to heaven which has been lost to us, as the Emerald Tablet which was given to us in its stead, as the human heart and the heart of God of which the Emerald's essence consists, and as the Grail Cup which the earth and her peoples must form together via a great unifying act of brotherhood and love in order to receive again the measureless wonder that was once given.

The paradox is that we must begin to reconnect individually in order for this to happen, and that the time to begin is now. This is why we need the Ka angels to help us on our way with the gentlest, entirely sanctioned and freely requested kick up the posterior, so that we avoid falling into a defile of atrophy and sleep!

The question remains, if we have the Emerald Tablet on earth, why can we not access its marvellous secrets and so begin to remedy the situation created by the loss of the Grail (the divine connection)? The answer is simple. Enlil could not destroy the Emerald Tablet, because its grade of being was too evolved for him to know how. But he could hide it.

And that was exactly what he did.

Chapter Thirteen

A CUNNING PLAN

The Emerald Tablet should have gone to Enki. He was the one due to inherit the kingship according to his rightful matrilineal claim. The Dragon Queen had actually given the Emerald Tablet into his safekeeping, as the Sumerian texts relate. But Enlil unlawfully seized the kingship, and denied it to his brother. As soon as this takeover had occurred, Enki was forced to relinquish the immeasurably precious Emerald Tablet into his brother's hands. Nevertheless, they retained duel governorship of it.

Knowing that Enlil was unable to hurt or destroy the stone and its records, Enki was not greatly concerned about its safety as long as it was visibly housed in Enlil's court, which was also his own home.

However, Enlil had a plan.

It was true that he could not harm the Emerald Tablet, nor could he hide it as, even though the Dragon Queen had been banished and reduced to anathema, the ever-present heart connection to her caused the Serpent People to cherish the fabulously beautiful stone of power and mystery that she had vouchsafed to them. Its disappearance would be met with great perturbation and an unending determination to discover its whereabouts. Yet the Stone had to go. While ever it remained accessible to the Serpent People, it was also accessible to the despised earthlings.

Enlil had no doubt that Enki and Nin-Khursag would continue to take their side and advance their evolution with its secrets. And its secrets were so powerful and profound that they assuredly would, in time, elevate the disgusting animal-bodied humans to the same level of glorious attainment as that enjoyed by proper humanity: the Serpent People. Enlil was determined that the Emerald Tablet, at all costs, should be removed.

He sought once again the help of his most important ally, the scientific genius whom he had consulted and collaborated with in the past. Together, they devised a plan. And it was a very cunning plan indeed.

Enlil would plot with his co-conspirators so that an apparent rumpus, a kind of coup, would take place within the Hall of Council over which he presided. Marduk, surreptitiously, would seize the Emerald Tablet and make off with it. Enlil would overpower the aggressors, who would submit to him and apologize for their actions. All would return to normal, except that Enlil would declare, in the gravest tones, that the Emerald Tablet had been lost in the fracas.

Meanwhile, Marduk would present the Emerald Tablet to the king Zi-u-Sudra, Enlil's scientist colleague. By ingenious method, by alchemical means most secret and devious, the Emerald Tablet would be hidden away in a concealed dimension that tricked the perception. No one would ever dream of the existence of this dimension, let alone consider searching it. The Emerald Tablet would be virtually under the noses of the Serpent People, and yet it would be absolutely locked away, invisible and irretrievable as it would be if every atom of it had been pulverized into nothing.

Besides, no one would search for it, because no one would

ever guess that it was missing. Enlil would triumphantly bear it back to court, claiming to have miraculously found it; for the scientific genius would create a fake but convincing Emerald Tablet for him to restore to the Serpent People in pomp and ceremony, into which a little of the original had been copied. There would be half-secrets, half-pointers, whispered intimations of the genuine article within its dimensions. It would appear to be the Emerald Tablet, but its essential integrity would be lost.

At this point, it would be Enlil's turn to set to work. Using his own genius for deception and malignant influence, Enlil would twist and corrupt some of those potencies within the fake Emerald Tablet that had been carried over from the true one until, instead of building bridges and setting humanity on the right road again, they sent it scurrying off into mires and pitfalls beyond description. The emanations from the Emerald Tablet would, thereby, rather than rescuing humankind from the abyss, lure it straight into the labyrinth until, stumbling and confused in the dark, it met the Minotaur at the heart of its distorted aspirations instead of the centre of divinity and spiritual consummation it supposed it was heading for. The Minotaur is the devourer of the soul and represents the unleashed and unadulterated forces of materialism. 'Matter is a force to be reckoned with!' declared Christ in Mary's gospel.

The plan was perfected and executed faultlessly. The Emerald Tablet was lost to the earth. The fake one was set up in its place, and began to do harm immediately.

Nevertheless, Cain and his descendants continued to maintain the secret 'underground stream' of knowledge relating to the Temple of Enki, which taught that Father God was born of Mother God and bowed his knee in reverence to the supremacy of the wisdom in the heart. Ham (Zarathustra) was the founder of the esoteric groups comprising this 'underground stream' with their emphasis on the power and significance of the Sacred Feminine.

The Manichaens, the Mandeans, the Bogomils, the Cathars, the Templars, the Masons, the Rosicrucians, the alchemists, and others, all had their root in this mystic tree whose origins branched back to the Dragon Queen herself. Not surprisingly, Enlil targeted these groups with all his might and main, managing to corrupt and confuse some and totally exterminate others.

It was Ham's teachings, linked with the true teachings of the Christ, which ushered in the Age of Chivalry with its stories of King Arthur and his woman-honouring knights, although my belief and confirmation is that these tales relate to a historical actuality that manifested in the sixth century. Scholars point out that Zoroaster's god was strictly masculine and bore no feminine aspect whatsoever, but this was simply because Zoroaster's god was Enki (a human being, but godlike or 'superhuman'), who had suffered from the Dolorous Blow in being cut off from his feminine counterpart, Nin-Khursag, with whom he would otherwise have shared an androgynous relationship. Her teachings were his, because he revered her and was linked to the Dragon Queen via her; besides which, all the groups emerging from the 'underground stream' enshrined secrets relating to the Sacred Feminine. The prevailing patriarchal culture, however, cast all female influence into shadow and near-invisibility.

Where Zoroastrianism became an outer, rigid structure, it took on some of the characteristics of Enlil, who managed to contaminate it and, in time, as mentioned, even many groups belonging to the 'underground stream' fell under his sway. Yet, where there were true devotees of the spirit of Zoroaster's teachings, such as within the ranks of the Balkan Bogomils ('Lovers of God'), there was always the deepest reverence and respect for women, who were considered guardians of secrets and mistresses of arcane lore that only their femininity could activate. Male supremacy was not a serious concept, although no doubt some cosmetic aspects of it persisted because of the cultural pressure of the times.

Ham (Zarathustra) did all he could to rectify the situation as far as correcting and purifying the teachings emanating from the Emerald Tablet were concerned. His own teachings continued unswervingly to honour his ancestor, the God of Light and Life, Ahura Mazda (Enki). The Zoroastrians that followed on from him elected their own High Priests, who continued down the centuries to be given the titular name of Zarathustra until Zoroastrianism became in its outer structure so usurped by Enlil that Enki withdrew it from the exterior world and permitted only the mysteries of its central core to continue. The name Khem-Zarathustra, however, was reserved solely for Ham, because 'Khem' denoted the real Emerald Tablet itself. While his knowledge and spiritual perception touched and reflected the essence of the true Emerald Tablet, it was inevitably the false one that Ham inherited, for inherit it he did, after Enlil's banishment (although his banishment does not prevent him from being powerfully manipulative behind the scenes).

And so, because of his inheritance, Ham was able to untangle and correct some of Enlil's damage to the partial teachings contained within the false Emerald Tablet, and restore some small part of the true version of its beauty and mystery.

However, even Ham and Enki together were not sufficiently exalted to rescue the vital and all-important genuine Emerald Tablet from its hiding-place, or to be privy to all of its secrets. A divine couple (Jesus and Mary Magdalene) were on their way to fulfil these quests, and after they did, their unconscionable gift could not be given to the world, because the world would not accept it. Hideous forces of the utmost evil massed to seize it once again. So the recovered Emerald Tablet was hidden away in a crypt in the grounds of Lincoln Cathedral (England) which, in those days, was less than six miles distant from the edge of the sacred Sherwood Forest, where there were guardians in place to ensure that it rested in safety. There it lies, waiting for the Ka angels to help us to prepare to receive it!

It is in the form of transcripts, as the emerald itself remains imprisoned in the dimension into which it was committed by malignant design so long ago. However, the vital key that we need in order to properly understand the teachings of Christ, and so together form the Grail Cup that will receive from heaven what we require to utterly transform ourselves and the earth forever, has been given to us within the pages of the sacred book that lies within the buried crypt.

Meanwhile, the false Emerald Tablet, despite Ham's best efforts, continued to do damage. While there were saving graces within its context due to his corrections, the terrible shadow of materialism, set there as a trap by Enlil, continued to pulse from it in death waves.

The latest rendition of it entered into the extremely popular book, *The Secret*, based on an interpretation of texts from the Emerald Tablet, which instructs its readers to enter more and more deeply into materialism via the most ancient alchemical and eternal laws. And yet materialism is the tomb that constricts us, and from which we desperately need to escape!

Mithra is the great angel who works directly with Enki, and all teachers of the light, to unbind us and lift us out of the crassness and deadliness of materialism. This is why he–she is the angel of unfading glory, the angel of ascension, and the angel of the Grail. Materialism makes our soul state heavy and sleepy and unable to ascend. But Mithra is standing by. Knowledge of Mithra is the golden gift entrusted to us by Enki, by Zarathustra. Mithra is an expression of the Christ principle, the angelic aspect of Christ consciousness, and indeed it was the earthly representatives of the Christ, Jesus and Mary Magdalene, who rescued for us the sacred knowledge contained within the true Emerald Tablet and, together with their teachings and revelations, took away the threat of hopelessness and ultimate death that hung over our world. They did, very literally, save us.

It is important to note that, although a sacred symbol and a teaching in its own right, it was not the crucifixion which killed Jesus, but the spear of Longinus, the Roman soldier who made the wound in the side of Christ that ran with blood and with water. In the sacrifice of his life to this death strike, Jesus reversed the evil magic of the Dolorous Blow, and simultaneously unlocked the dimension in which the Emerald Tablet had been so deeply hidden.

Because of their profound closeness in spirit, Jesus and Mary Magdalene created a polarity between the higher and the earthly planes. They remained in intimate communion despite their apparent separation. Via this beautiful 'satellite link', Jesus was able to read the Emerald Tablet with the help of Mary, who spoke the divine words it stored within its essence as their conjoined consciousness became consummate with its knowledge. John, faithful servant of the divine couple and brother to Mary, made transcripts as Mary spoke, so that a book was created, often called 'the Lost Gospel of John' or 'The Book of Love', for intimations and whispers of its existence have persisted down the centuries. Mystical sects of Johannite Christians, especially the Templars whose order arose from a contingent of high-ranking Druids that became Culdee monks, knew a little of what it contained, as did the Cathars.

Yet no earthly group or individual so far, except Mary Magdalene, John, and Tamar, the daughter of Jesus and Mary in whom the mystery of the Holy Grail ultimately resides (see references to Derdekea in Chapter 19, *The Faceless Woman*) has ever entered into the full revelation of the true Emerald Tablet. This hoard of ineffable and unconscionable treasure lies waiting to be recovered at the site of Lincoln cathedral.

Having now reached an understanding of the history of Zarathustra and his great ministering angel, Mithra, we can begin to enter into the Mithraic rites.

Chapter Fourteen

THE GOLDEN TWIN

One essential before embarking on the Mithraic rites is to understand that each ceremony is designed so that the invocant may receive angelic gifts and, most importantly, that the gifts requested must not be selfish gifts. We receive spiritual gifts from Mithra. For instance, we may feel in need of courage and strength, perhaps to escape from a situation created by those of ill-intent. It is good to ask for courage and strength both to rise above and transform that situation, but unacceptable to ask for courage and strength to crush our enemies. Mithra bestows gifts only on the kind and loving heart that is seeking attunement to its God-self. We do not wish to rouse the Minotaur.

Asking for material gifts is also a mistake. We can ask for blessing and balance, for blockages to our well-being to be cleared and cleansed, and for guidance to help us through difficult times, of course. But the main function and focus of the Mithraic ceremonies are to release us into our higher self. Mithra is the angel of ascension, the angel of the Grail. He releases us from materialism and will not help to embed us in it.

Of course, it is not selfish to ask for help to overcome addictions, such as binge-drinking or overeating, or for other forms of healing. Getting rid of such burdens is well within the Mithraic remit.

It is a good idea to come to Mithra cleansed and prepared before we seek to receive his golden dynamic influence. Chalchiuhtlicue (see Chapter Two) will spin through us like a laughing whirlpool and cast out heavy, uncreative energy. Vwyamus will clear our soul channels and banish unpleasant thought-matter. You might prefer simply to call on the angels of cleansing rather than named angels, or to do both.

Calling on the Angels

Just follow these ten simple steps:

Find a quiet place, or withdraw deep into the privacy and quietude within yourself.

Let your focus gently touch your heart, and allow your mind to rest there.

In an act of imagination, let your breath rise and fall through your heart.

Breathe slowly and easily, letting the rhythm of your breath bring you peace.

Let that point of peace fill you with light as if it were a shining star.

Ask for the protection of Archangels Michael and Shekinah.

Make a request to your guardian angel to be linked safely, securely and harmoniously with any Ka angel you might be working with.

Put out a call from your heart to a named angel, or to the individual angel or group of angels that serve and ensoul the principle you seek (the angel or angels of cleansing, for instance).

Spell out very clearly (if it is not possible to speak aloud, say the words with great precision in your mind, and hear yourself speaking them) exactly what it is that you want the angels to do for you.

Thank the angels for the gifts you are about to receive.

It is also beneficial to call on Haamiah or the angel of truth before beginning Mithraic rites. Amitiel, Gabriel and Michael are guardians of the spirit of truth, so Haamiah may be summoned in conjunction with them.

Your preparation might be ordered along these lines:

Sitting quietly, you have withdrawn into the depths of yourself. You bring your heart centre into focus and allow your mind to sink softly into your heart. You breathe easily and gently, a little more slowly than usual. Via an act of intention, you allow your breath to rise and fall through your heart.

Listening to and feeling the soothing rhythm of your breath, you relax into peace. You feel the peace create a bright point, which fills you with light.

You ask for protection by saying, 'Archangel Michael, Archangel Shekinah, protect me and this ceremony throughout its duration.' You call first on Chalchiuhtlicue (you can abbreviate her name to 'Chalchi' if you prefer). Sending forth a silent appeal from your heart, you think of her qualities and feel her surround you with a torrent of washing, laughing, cleansing energy.

You say, aloud or in your mind, 'Chalchiuhtlicue, please cleanse and prepare me for the coming ceremony with the power of your purifying energies.' You maintain your heart link with Chalchiuhtlicue for a moment or two while she fulfils your request.

You now repeat the procedure with Vwyamus, first putting out the silent call from your heart and then wording your request by saying, 'Vwyamus, please decongest all my channels of consciousness and energy with your radiant forces of cleansing in preparation for the coming ceremony.'

Remain briefly linked with the mighty angel Vwyamus, who melts away resistance to the light as the rising sun melts away obscuring mists and vapour.

You move on now to the angels of truth, who are Gabriel, Amitiel, Michael and Haamiah.

These four angels form a golden pyramid coruscating with light. Strangely enough, you see that all four are present at each point of the four-square base of the pyramid, and at its apex. Ascend the pyramid by mounting a golden stair to its summit. Held in its pinnacle of light, you call on the angels of truth to be present in your heart, and then enunciate, 'Gabriel, Amitiel, Haamiah, Michael, great angels of Truth, surround me with the strength and clarity of your light and be with me throughout this ceremony.'

Thank the angels for their loving service to you.

You are now ready to begin.

When we come into the presence of Mithra, we come into the presence of the divine fire of God. He is an emission of a great light that extends beyond the frontiers of our imagination, and yet speaks to us of our limitlessness. The light, which is love, is imbued with countless qualities, but when we are within the aura of Mithra we are especially aware that we can forge ourselves anew.

The First Mithraic Rite

The ceremony is simple. First put out a call from the heart, and then summon Mithra by saying his name in gentle rhythm three times. (The name is pronounced with a short 'i' followed by 'ra' as in Ra, the Egyptian sun god.)

Feel the glory of Mithra, like spiritual gold of the utmost brilliance, descend on you and surround you entirely.

Imagine a round mirror. It can be as big as you like.

Look into its depths.

See your own reflection therein, yet see it as a reflection in gold. It is you, glowing with a radiance of purest gold; yourself, but golden.

This is your golden twin. See your twin smile and take both your hands.

Whatever quality you feel you are lacking or wish to aspire to, see it shining from your twin. The essence of your golden twin expresses the quality in perfection. You can see it in the eyes, in the smile, of your twin; in the energy of the golden brilliance your twin is throwing off. Your twin is you, your golden reflection.

Look deep into the mirror.

Now the illumination from Mithra, like the perfect light of morning in a dream of Paradise, melts away the dimensions of the mirror so that nothing separates you from your twin. Your twin strengthens your mutual handclasp and you ascend into the heavens, into that point of brightest celestial light that is the same as the light in your heart.

Here, absorbed into the point of God's heart where you can forge yourself anew, into the source of *prana* or 'dragon-fire', your divine twin merges with you and you become one. The quality you seek is infused into you. You breathe it in, and it is yours.

Gently reconnect with the earth by sitting quietly for a moment and imagining strong roots, like tree roots, growing down from the soles of your feet into the ground until they reach the heart of the earth. Let them anchor firmly there.

See a vivid white-silver cross in a ring of light touch and glow out from each of your main chakras: the crown of your head, the top of your forehead at its centre point, the brow ridge above your nose, the hollow of your throat, your heart, your solar plexus, just below your navel and the bottom of your spine at the point of the tail bone.

End the ceremony by thanking Mithra and the angels for their ministrations.

Many times throughout the day, even if just for a moment, let your thoughts turn to your golden twin. See your twin radiant and smiling, with loving, encouraging eyes, ascending into heaven and showing you the raised, exalted, golden reflection of yourself perfectly expressing the quality you seek. Breathe it in and claim it as your own. Identify with your golden twin.

You will find that eventually you cannot feel doubtful of yourself or in any way negative or disillusioned about yourself, because your divine twin is golden and perfect in the heavens, showing you that you are already everything you aspire to be, borne up by the light of Mithra into the grace of God.

Use this ceremony to work on one quality at a time, or two allied qualities such as strength and courage, until you feel there has been a complete absorption.

The Second Mithraic Rite

The second Mithra ceremony is just as simple. Prepare for it as for the one above, and call on Mithra three times in gentle rhythm.

Feel the descent of the glorious angel Mithra as he surrounds you with a vast aura of gold. His vivid presence settles gently into your heart.

Through Mithra's divine ministrations, feel yourself

blending with the bright light of the sun, and then with the golden rays of the spiritual sun that is behind the manifesting universe.

Let the light absorb you and, simultaneously, allow yourself to absorb the healing celestial rays of the spiritual sun into your heart. Focus on your breath, knowing that your breath is magical. Your breath will work the Mithraic magic.

Breathe in the life-giving, life-affirming, life-sustaining rays of the spiritual sun and know that they are entering deeply into every chakra (the series of points listed above, which are sealed at the close of a ceremony with the white-silver cross in a ring of light), into every nerve, cell and tissue of your body, and deep into the spiritual atoms of your being. Feel this supreme luminosity permeate every spiritual and physical particle of your body. See these spiritual atoms within you light up like a galaxy of brilliant stars throwing off unutterable radiance; and yet they are in your shape, and are you. You have become a being of the golden sunlight. Live and thrive on these sparkling golden spiritual atoms that pour into you from the sun and cause your own spiritual atoms to take fire and coruscate with the divine fire of God. Breathe them in and claim your sacred Pendragonship. Spend a little time enjoying this divine communion.

Now breathe one relaxed, full cycle of breath to a count of three (in and out once, three beats to the in-breath and three beats to the out-breath).

Affirm:

'I dwell solely upon the power of the golden sun that courses through me with every healing breath. I am in perfect control of my thoughts.'

Repeat the breath cycle and affirm:

'I am in perfect control of my nervous energy. I am calm

and poised in the heart of the sun, where only good
can be.'

Repeat the breath cycle and affirm:

'I know that the secret of the sun and the secret of the
heart of God is love.'

Repeat the breath cycle and affirm:

'Honouring this knowledge, I am now imbued with the
power to master my life.'

Repeat the final breath cycle and affirm:

'I am filled with the sun. I bathe in a floodtide of golden
consciousness. I am healed. I am whole.'

Maintain your connection to Mithra, the sun, and God's heart
for a few moments.

Gently reconnect with the earth by imagining strong
roots, like tree roots, growing down from the soles of your
feet into the ground until they reach the heart of the earth.
See them anchor firmly there.

As before, envision a vivid white-silver cross in a ring of
light touch and glow out from your chakras: the crown
of your head, the top of your forehead at its centre point,
the brow ridge above your nose, the hollow of your throat,
your heart, your solar plexus, just below your navel and the
bottom of your spine at the point of the tail bone.

Complete the ceremony by thanking Mithra and the
angels for their ministrations.

This ceremony can be used for your healing and regenera-
tion, and to gain strength, balance and poise. If you have a
specific condition, send the spiritual sunlight to the point of
affliction and feel the great spirit of love which is the radiation of the magical sunlight entirely surround and absorb
it. Perform the ceremony every day. As the days and weeks

pass, you will begin to sense healing on many levels.

The two ceremonies do not have to be enacted together. You can choose to perform either at any time, or both of them in any sequence as you wish. Of course, you do not need to go through the entire ceremonial procedure to call on Mithra once you have performed the rites and touched his essence. You can call on him directly at any time and enter into the magic circle of his golden strength and purity.

It is worth repeating that avoiding any selfish or abusive use of these ceremonies is essential for your happiness and safety. Mithra is an almighty Ka angel, and we cannot mess with the Ka angels!

Chapter Fifteen

VOHU MANAH, ANGEL OF GOOD THOUGHT

Now we have acquainted ourselves with Mithra the Glorious, and examined to some extent the kind of pitfalls and traps that the darkness sets for human consciousness, we can progress through the influences of the other mighty Ka angels. After Mithra, Vohu Manah, Angel of Good Thought, is the first port of call in our vital work of inviting in the Ka angels and learning how to live our lives in close communion with them.

Attuning to the Ka angels is a very definite decision to make in life; a path which is chosen deliberately and carefully. They present themselves at this point and in this guise because of the treasure of potential locked into the extremity of the times. The Ka angels joyfully anticipate helping us wholly to realize that potential and to fulfil our soul qualities and healing needs with its abundant gifts. Those gifts will enable us more fully to give our own gifts to the world, for the world stands in need of them.

To do this, we have to make a push at this juncture in a way that has never been required of us, en masse, before. It is a spiritual push, a spiritual leap, that we must make in order to achieve the breakthrough that beckons. To utilize anything other than our spiritual will and wisdom and the higher love of the heart would result in missing the mark;

and missing the mark could well prove to be both destructive and painful. Therefore, before advancing deeper into Ka angel 'territory', it is important to prepare ourselves, our soul-vehicles, for the journey.

The principle of 'good thought' and its overlighting angel Vohu Manah constitutes an excellent starting-point. As with the entire angelic realm, Vohu Manah works not only for the personal good of the invocant, but for the good of the whole. This seems to be especially relevant in the case of the Ka angels, for they are working for the good of all creation on a majestic scale. Lowly though we may be on this planet, humble though our level of evolution and present advancement undoubtedly is, if we go down and are lost as a collective vehicle of individual souls striving to bring forth the light through ourselves, the whole of creation will feel the destruction and the reversal, and will suffer the repercussions.

Therefore, the chance to work with the Ka angels at this time bears an unprecedented promise within its wings: the chance to reach heights unparalleled and the chance to further all creation by our own individual effort. When we think in these terms, the idea of striving only for ourselves and our own personal advantage begins to seem an unworthy, blinkered, poor and mean-spirited aspiration. Our canvas can be as wide as the heavens; our efforts can be God-enhanced. This is how we feel true joy.

Before we can understand Vohu Manah, we need to understand the mighty power of thought itself. If, indeed, there are two great principles – good and evil – at work in life, as Zoroaster tells us, then the forces of thought in particular work through them to create good or ill in our lives and in the world at large. We can use the power of the two interconnecting wheels of light and darkness or good and evil (although there are positive and negative aspects of both darkness and light) to create either paradisiacal or hellish conditions. An absolute requisite of the former is to attune to good thought.

We can perhaps misunderstand this principle sometimes. It seems to be unhelpful, for instance, to cling to the idea of good thought in a kind of hysterical denial of the darkness and insist that 'everything in the garden is lovely'. That is really more an expression of fear and an unwillingness to deal with the darkness we encounter in life, which of course gives it greater power. The trick is rather to transform darkness as it appears.

To take an extreme example, you might have a young family and live in an area where a convicted paedophile has been resettled. Attuning to good thought, you believe that this person's soul can begin to heal and turn to the light, and accordingly with the aid of the angels you send forth good, helpful, positive thought-structures, always seeing the integrity of the person's soul being restored and believing in that soul's innate goodness.

At the same time, you would of course be careful not to expose your children to any vulnerable situation involving that person, and would cast a ring of protective light around your own and other children in the neighbourhood. The light you summon would arise from love, and would help the afflictions of the struggling soul as well as serving to protect the children. If there was the slightest suspicion that the paedophile was again becoming active, naturally you would immediately inform the authorities and, while entirely condemning the malignant and destructive urges involved, you would send a blessing to that maimed soul and continue to believe that it could break out of its darkness. This would be an expression of attunement to good thought.

To compress a point, good thought does not involve over-optimism, but rather shrewd assessment couched in non-condemnation of people (not actions) and a visionary faith in the best outcome, which together comprise a beautiful and potent force that has nothing to do with blindness, denial or excuse. Without shrewd assessment, we would be unable to determine which components of good thought were needed in any particular case.

Would the application of good thought described above really transform the particularly distressing darkness identified as paedophile tendencies? What it would certainly do is to protect the tenderness of children's auras from the onslaught of the harm generated by such predatory instincts, even when they are not practically active, and to ensure that the perpetrator was not pushed even further into the jaws of his or her own darkness but rather offered a hand out of it. It is true that the proffered hand may not always be taken. Nevertheless, as we build the power of good thought in our world, the likelihood increases that, one day, it will be decisively grasped.

Of course, not all darkness is as stubborn and unrelenting as that relating to such painful problems. The attunement to good thought will undoubtedly bring harmony and beauty and delight into our lives. We can deal with the darkness while securing ourselves in a place of faith and happiness within, peacefully projecting thoughts that bless and thoughts that summon only good and blessed outcomes, while refraining from in any way mentating what these should actually be. We ourselves can only be partial judges, so we create a problem when we try to force the flow of reality into a rigid framework of our own limited construction, however well intended the measure.

Instead, we allow the dynamics of the spirit, of higher consciousness, to do this work, and we play our part by simply contributing the force of good thought to the situation. This is where Vohu Manah waits to serve us.

Vohu Manah teaches us that good thought is not the same as positive thinking, although of course the two bear certain similarities. Positive thinking usually involves trying to make something specific happen, virtually as an act of will by powerfully believing that thought, visualization and belief itself can bring what is desired into manifestation. Although there may be an element of this from a certain standpoint as part of the admixture of 'good thought', essentially the two are very different.

'Good thought' is softly generated by the heart poised in peace and radiance that recognizes the principle of love as the only master to which it bears allegiance. It rests in the knowledge that all works together to create good and to bring the balm of healing and resolution to the horrors that the world produces. This is no passive stance, however. 'Good thought' is part of the God-force in life, and it works actively to bring about the healing, resolution and happiness to which it is attuned. Good thought in itself can bring about a joyful outcome, sometimes almost miraculously. Generating good thought is to charge a situation with magical power: the power of good thought; the power of Vohu Manah.

It may be helpful to bear in mind some of the important truths about the power of thought, which have been communicated to us down the ages by spiritual masters and angelic teachers.

Thought is one of the most potent creative forces in the universe. As yet, humanity truly has no idea how powerful it is, and how dramatically our lives and circumstances respond to it.

Our thoughts are not our own. We are receiving and transmitting stations, attracting thought-streams and thought-qualities according to the vibrations of our subtle bodies (emotional, mental, intuitional, etc.). We perpetuate, create and generate our own thoughts from what arrives at the door of our palace of thought, bad and good, from sources other than ourselves via the law of attraction.

When we invite Vohu Manah into our palace of thought, it becomes easier to transform or reject the unhappy, anxious, inappropriate, destructive, chaotic or angry thoughts and to retain and breathe even more vital life into the good, healing, happy and beautiful thoughts that we receive.

To see nothing but good (without irresponsibility) and to focus on a good and happy outcome is a very powerful contribution towards achieving that happy outcome.

To send fearful, anxious thoughts to a person or a situation actually aggravates the negative situation.

To send loving, positive thoughts of well-being, thoughts of healing and protection and faith that all is well, is a very real, active and definite contribution you can make to the situation of someone in distress and danger. There is, after all, something you can do.

Demeaning thoughts or critical thoughts make their way through the ethers to their target and, especially if that person is in a vulnerable state, can be as destructive as if they were dinned in the ears of the recipient or as if some germ in them took invasive root, having a real impact on their morale and confidence and their ability to cope or steer what they are doing to a successful conclusion.

If you find that you have allowed yourself to send out negative thoughts of any kind, you can always redress the balance by immediately cancelling out the thought-package (*see* page 153), asking the angels to heal the malignancy and sending out a thought-ship packed with provisions of love and support instead.

We are constantly building our world, our environment and what materializes within it with the power of our thoughts. The control and positive use of thought is one of life's most vital lessons.

Faith is the potency of good thought. Faith in beauty and goodness and the power of love to overcome all things is magical. Faith does not involve foolishness or blindness; it is not blinkered denial, but rather a great God-power that lifts earthly conditions into an unlimited shining realm beyond the constrictions of earthly law and earthly reality. We become a mighty powerhouse when we can generate this exalted faith. We become the stillness at the heart of the storm. A thousand may fall to our right, and a thousand again to our left, but when we stand in the light of this golden faith, we are unassailed. We become a great pillar of steadfastness and shielding for others as well as ourselves.

When the negative thought is random or unexpected and is an isolated manifestation, rather than the barrage of distressing thoughts described below, you can 'pop' it! Just see (and even hear) it pop, and from its mini-explosion see a star arise, a star of blessing to which you can give wings and direct to the person or situation you have blasted with your negative thought. It will rectify the situation and charge its target with light.

Of course, it is all very well to say, 'Don't have negative

thoughts; always throw them out.' Sometimes, an inner state of fear, depression and deep unhappiness seems to spontaneously generate a thought flow that constantly reflects the indwelling condition. Turning off or turning away this thought stream can be like trying to turn off consciousness itself.

Vohu Manah can come to our aid in such circumstances. This almighty angel enfolds us in great wings of softest blue, like a perfect summer sky. Vohu Manah actually gathers us up into the blue, as though we are taken right into the eternal deeps of the smiling blue sky. I think that the person who coined the current phrase 'blue sky thinking' is in vivid touch with Vohu Manah!

If you suffer from a condition of distress that seems to generate its own continuous thought-flow of misery or perhaps vexed criticism of life and people, you can move back into inner peace and harmony through Vohu Manah. You may encounter resistance in surrendering this thought-flow, especially as there will almost inevitably be an element of anger within the energy of its unhappy and protesting emission. It can be very difficult to move away from this anger, because it can seem self-protective, as though without it we would have no force of will and might become weak, passive and easy prey, and that there would be no voice any more to speak up for us and our unhappiness.

We can be very sure, however, that Vohu Manah will not allow us to be bereft in this way, but will transfigure inner conditions so that our will, becoming re-attuned to our harmonious and peaceful spiritual will, is returned to its proper potency; and that no frightening area of inward misery is left unprotected, because it will be transformed into an inner strength.

Before beginning the ceremonies to Vohu Manah, it is helpful to say several times aloud as a mantra of peace the following simple words from St Theresa of Avila.

> Let nothing disturb thee;
> Let nothing dismay thee;
> All things pass;
> God never changes;
> Patience attains all that it strives for;
> They who have God find they lack nothing;
> God alone suffices.

And from Christ:

> Let not your heart be troubled;
> nor let it be afraid.
> My peace I give unto thee;
> My peace I leave with thee.

Having attuned to the blue calmness of Vohu Manah, it is time to return to the Brothers Grimm for more enlightenment. I am always mindful of their name, for in the 'rabbit language' it is tantalizingly suggestive of 'grimoire', the magical source-book from which occultists anciently drew their knowledge and understanding of angels, nature spirits and demons, adding to it with their own compilations as their experience increased. A grimoire was a form of record-keeping for the soul, a book of intrinsic knowledge. Likewise, the annals of the Brothers Grimm give forth this knowledge, to those with ears to hear, of the darkness and the light, of the supernal and the subterranean realms.

The fairytale in this instance that would leap into that dreamscape of the heart, which is the human delight in the power of story, is called 'Mother Frost'. I believe that it is the magical element in frost that the title and its subject highlight: the tiny, exquisite atoms comprising frost, which are six-pointed stars of crystalline light shining with a pure unearthly brilliance as of supernatural diamonds. 'Mother Frost' is the Mother of Light, the Mother of Good Thought, of thoughts of the creative light. These frost crystals, of themselves, have a beautiful and astounding story to tell of the God-like power of thoughts and words, which is revealed in Chapter 20.

Mother Frost is also Mother Goose, the feminine source of all the wisdom of fairytale, myth and dream. Like Vohu Manah, she dwells in a secret dimension within the blue heavens. There are many old stories springing from the same root, telling of a mysterious mother in the sky who plucks magical goose-feathers and sends them down as snow. Again, it is the mystery of the snow; its six-pointed starry atoms, which are the focus for meaning, for they are vehicles of the white light of heaven that is also within us and that gives each one of us our dragon inheritance of the pure, magical light of God with which we can stupendously create the world anew. The goose feathers represent the gentle touch of wisdom, of enlightenment, that the starry atoms bring.

Considered in our current culture as foolish and generally 'silly', the goose was once a revered and redoubtable symbol of maternity, of Mother God. Last century the bronze figurine of a Celtic war goddess was found in Brittany wearing a helmet surmounted by a goose in combative posture.

Near Bosnia, home of the Bogomils ('lovers of God') who spawned the mysterious Cathars and who, like them, bore secrets within their esoteric culture relating to the Temple of Enki or Oannes/John and therefore of Mother God, the tombs of Iron Age warriors, who had been ritualistically interred with the sacred goose, have been discovered.

Mother Frost

The Brothers Grimm story begins with two sisters living in a wood with a woman who is mother to one and step-mother to the other. One of the daughters is attuned to the spirit and follows the lead of her soul. The other is given over entirely to worldliness. The mother is a figure we meet often in fairytale and myth – the False or the Dark Mother, called Mammon in the Bible. She is the mother of the worldly daughter in the story, and a cruel stepmother to the daughter who listens to her soul.

From the point of view of Enki's story, we might recognize her as the dead, dark image of womanhood held up for us after the Dolorous Blow. It is a fake image, of course, for the Dark Mother lacks the Mother's true essence of the most royal and sacred dragon fire. Through our own ignorance, the False Mother leads us into the depths of materialism rather than into the heart of the mysteries of ascension.

And so the three live together in their cottage in the wood, the soulful stepdaughter acting as skivvy for her stepmother and stepsister, who both abuse her. One morning, while drawing water for the household, she hears a voice calling to her from within the well. Leaning too far over in her curiosity, she falls in, and finds herself in a heavenly world. Wandering delightedly through perfect meadows filled with exquisite flowers, she comes across a little house that shines like gold. From within its bright walls, she hears again the voice she had heard at the lip of the well.

Going inside, she finds an angelic old woman who

introduces herself as Mother Frost. The old woman asks the girl to work for her, promising her fair wages, and bidding her to be careful to shake the mattress of the old woman's bed very well every morning, because the action dispenses blessings to the earth world below.

The girl agrees, and does the work of the house for several weeks. She sings as she works, takes care to attend to everything that needs doing, and is scrupulous about shaking out Mother Frost's mattress each morning, watching the silver-bright goose-down fall to the earth below as feathery blessings while she does so. In the evenings, when Mother Frost returns home from her wanderings through heaven, she sits at her knee and listens to her wisdom until bedtime. The girl has recognized Mother Frost as her true mother, the Mother of All Souls.

One day, Mother Frost tells her it is time to return to her own world, and directs her through a mysterious gate. As she passes under the gate, a shower of fragrant filaments of the purest gold descends on her and clings to her from head to foot. She becomes a shining maiden, alight with a golden aura of marvellous beauty. Exclaiming in surprise as the gold descends and enfolds her, she finds that precious jewels issue from her mouth each time she speaks.

She returns to her home and is greeted with wonder. She shares her experiences with her stepmother and stepsister. Raging with jealousy, the stepmother thinks, 'If all she did was to fall down a well, my own daughter can do that.' So the daughter of the stepmother jumps down the well shaft and finds herself in the heavenly world. She passes through the fields of flowers, but takes no notice of them.

When she is invited to work for Mother Frost, she agrees, but is disconsolate and rails against her work, neglecting most of it and performing the rest very sketchily and with bad grace. She never shakes the mattress each morning as she has been asked.

When Mother Frost returns home each evening from her work in the heavens, the girl refuses to sit at her knee to listen to her wisdom, but is sullenly silent and dozes by the fire, thinking only of her release from service and the rewards she will be given. She will not allow Mother Frost to call forth from her her deeper soul, the source and expression of all her latent beauty, grace, wisdom and strength, and does not recognize the ancient angelic woman as her true mother.

In time, Mother Frost tells her she may return home. The girl roughly demands her pay, and Mother Frost assures her that it will be given in due measure. She instructs the girl to pass through the strange gate that leads back to her own world, but when she does so, a flood of foul-smelling pitch empties onto her. She shouts out in dismay, only to find that loathsome swamp creatures crawl out of her mouth with every word she utters. In this sorry state, she returns home.

On the face of it, this story seems conventionally moralistic, with a somewhat spiteful demonstration of just desserts. However, the Grimm stories have revealed themselves as a repository of angelic teachings as well as disclosing different strains of wisdom from other perspectives. And the angels, in particular Vohu Manah, do not view this story in the light of a dreary moralistic teaching at all, but in that of a very pragmatic demonstration of inner reality. They are keen to show us what really happens when we attune to good thought, and the deluge of distastefulness and misery we visit on ourselves when we ignore this vital need for the energetic, motivating force of good thought and constantly immerse ourselves in its opposite expression.

All the vivid pictorial information is there within the context of the story – the thoughts themselves forming words that are like precious jewels or slimy swamp creatures and the aura of gold that throws forth radiance and sweetness contrasted with the murky, dirty aura that gives off a noisome vibration. Both conditions, of course, activate the law of attraction accordingly, although the angels counsel us to focus more on what we are giving out rather than on what we receive.

As we enter into the rites of Vohu Manah, it helps to really absorb the impact of this story and recognize its counselling voice, not as a moralistic diatribe but as snapshot evidence of inner reality. When we feel the disturbing pressure within our consciousness of everything that assumes the proportions of 'bad thought', we can immediately begin to transform that waking nightmare by receiving and claiming our shining golden aura and sending it forth to the root of the disturbance. The little ceremonies dedicated to Vohu Manah facilitate and empower us in doing so. War zones, famines and disasters can be helped in this way, as well as endemic problems and aspects of our personal lives and relationships.

It sounds fanciful, yet it works. Of course, when we are conducting the forces of 'good thought' with our angelic self or that within us which responds to and resonates with the angels, the magic we create arises from that deepest self and not from a level that might be judged infantile, fanciful and trite. We are not playing an indulgent game, but commanding reality at its most vital level. It is important to bear this in mind as you prepare to perform the rites of Vohu Manah and the other Ka angels.

Chapter Sixteen

THE RITES OF VOHU MANAH

The rites of Vohu Manah, like those associated with all the Ka angels, are simple and unassuming. They each begin in the same way as the others:

The Rites

Find a quiet place, or withdraw deep into the privacy and quietude within yourself.

Let that point of peace fill you with light as if it were a shining star.

Ask for the protection of Archangels Michael and Shekinah.

Make a request to your guardian angel to be linked safely, securely and harmoniously with Vohu Manah.

Let your focus gently touch your heart, and allow your mind to rest there.

In an act of imagination, let your breath rise and fall through your heart.

Breathe slowly and easily, letting the rhythm of your breath bring you peace.

Know that your breath is magical, and will take you deep into the heart of the angelic realm.

Call on Vohu Manah by intoning her name softly three times. Begin to be taken up into the blue sky, a sky of the purest, happiest blue, deep and rich and luminous as if of angelic essence. Allow yourself to be absorbed into this sweet, heavenly blue, and become aware that you are in the heart of Vohu Manah.

As you look deep into the blue of Vohu Manah, a most beautiful cleansing of your eyes takes place. They gently relax, and become filled with Vohu Manah's blue, so that whatever the colour of your eyes, they are now one with the skies: an exquisite, shining blue.

At the centre of the brow ridge, your third eye opens onto this perfect blue. Your two eyes and your third eye make a pyramid, a flawless vehicle for sight.

Look deep, deeper, into the blue. There is a lake at its heart, clear as purity. Feel yourself being drawn into this lake of heaven.

At the heart of the lake shines a tranquil star. It is the star of the centre of your own being. Walk into its perfect light.

The heart of the star is your own heart. It has six points and it shines with your own essence, the starlight in your heart that is of God. The star is many things, but it is also the temple of Vohu Manah, of good thought. Feel yourself radiate good thought, the power of blessing, from each of the six points of the star. You are safe in its centre, its seventh point.

Now that you have become acquainted with the essence and the temple of Vohu Manah, you can continue with her rites or rest at this point and return to them later. If you would prefer to end the ceremony, bring it to a close in the usual way:

Gently reconnect with the earth by sitting quietly for a moment and imagining strong roots, like tree roots, growing down from the soles of your feet into the ground until they reach the heart of the earth. Let them anchor firmly there.

See a vivid white-silver cross in a ring of light touch and glow out from the crown of your head, the top of your forehead at its centre point, the brow ridge above your nose, the hollow of your throat, your heart, your solar plexus, just below your navel and at the bottom of your spine at the point of the tail bone.

End the ceremony by thanking Vohu Manah for her ministrations.

To continue with the rites, use the benefit of the ceremony given above to realize your absolute security and centredness in the magical six-pointed star as you progress.

You are in the temple of Vohu Manah, in the temple of the star.

As you dwell in peace in the heart of the star, know with a deep knowledge that you are in its centre, that its centre is your heart, and that, miraculously, the star also shines above you in the heavens, so that you can gaze into its guiding light.

Feel a shower of precious sunlight fall upon you like a mystical rain. It is falling from the star of wonder above. It is imbued with the magic of the light-essence within your heart, the golden secret behind the sunlight. It softly enfolds you like raiment, and surrounds you with a light of measurelessly beautiful gold, softly shining, yet incalculably bright. It is your gift of gold from the heart of the Divine.

It is your Pendragon essence. Delight in it; draw it around you, feel it emanating from deep within you. Know that it is not only a garment of light, but a revelation of your deepest self. Magically, it is a cloak that reveals you, that unleashes your light from its imprisonment. It is a soundless statement, unutterably true, that you are a child of light, a being of ineffable light. You are God's dream made real, stepping through the mirror.

Know that this gift of light that surrounds you, delicate as filigree but strong as the arm of God, is your shield and your tower that enfolds you by day and by night. It is invulnerable. Nothing can pierce it. And yet it sends light forth, in a radiance that is sometimes white, sometimes clear, sometimes golden, wherever you direct it to go.

However much light you send forth, its integrity is never breached or weakened, and it never grows less.

It goes forth with your breath; it goes forth with your thought. And its source is the star, which is your heart and the heart of God.

Of your own volition, you can send out that marvellous light to all people, all creatures, to any living being, to all situations, crises, or experiences of joy and creativity that loved ones, acquaintances or strangers, might be embarking upon. It is a blessing of the richest, rarest gold. It is your golden essence, your light, and it is sent forth in the form of a shining star, a star of your own blessed Pendragon radiance, which is the breath and the being of God.

You can send it forth endlessly. If thought-forms of limitation, of weariness, try to interpose themselves between you and your God-essence, invoke Vohu Manah simply and directly, by calling on her and thinking of the ethereal blue of the skies and the enfoldment of her wings.

This angel marshal of good thought will take you into the eternal depths of your being for replenishment and awakening, where your eyes will be cleansed and will open onto the everlasting vistas of spirit, the source that never runs dry or knows weariness. She will lead you to your powerhouse and treasure store of infinite gold, which can only come into manifestation if it is continually and freely given away with an open hand.

There, in the depths of the star of your being, you will enter into full cognizance that sending out the light in this way, sending forth good thought, constructive thought, blessing thought, breathing your mystical Pendragon essence out into the world, is effortless. It is activated by our spiritual will, with which we do have to make an effort to connect; but its keystone is unobstructed effortlessness.

It is God's essence, and we would never think of it egotistically as our 'own' power. Yet, magically, it is also your individual essence, and you will enter into its full potency by thinking of it in this way.

Be absorbed into the blue, find your golden raiment, shine from the centre of your star, and enter into the perfect peace and serene effortlessness of sending forth swathes of good thought like the northern lights, dancing across the thought-atmosphere of our world like great robes of joy.

End by thanking Vohu Manah for her ministrations.

Inevitably, there will be times when you feel imprisoned within an entirely different level of consciousness: earth-bound, uninspired, and perhaps disenchanted and impatient with the idea of the spiritual dimensions, which might occasionally seem wearying, demanding, unattractive and essentially irrelevant. At these hard times when the mind of earth tyrannically asserts its dominion, repeated calls to the angels, and to Vohu Manah, will eventually achieve a breakthrough. And there are several brief and simple rites associated with Voh Humanah designed to help us through difficult times.

The first of these is the use of the violet flame. This is well known, especially via the works of Elizabeth Clare Prophet.

The Ceremony of the Violet Flame

When negative thoughts overtake you, lasso them back. Send out a lasso of magical silver rope as they head out into the ether, loop them round and sweep them back. Imagine they are floating before you in the silver loop. Dissolve them in the purity of the violet flame, which cleanses and eradicates negativity. Just see a column of flame, of a deep and beautiful violet, gently engulf them, leap up, and burn with an even deeper, clearer violet hue. However, an energy vacuum is against natural and spiritual law, so it is important afterwards to send out the light of the six-pointed star in the heart to the person (or situation) to whom your thoughts were originally directed. Ask Vohu Manah's blessing and ministration on the entire ritual.

The Handclasp

When an attack of the lower mind comes on, and you are flooded with thoughts that carry a negative or even destructive energy (also see the next chapter), call on Vohu Manah for help very loudly and urgently. You will receive a handclasp. Take it and hang on. Sometimes you will just feel a beautiful inflow of warm and stable reassurance, as if a hush of deep peace enfolded you into its heart. At other times you will feel Vohu Manah ushering in an encompassing light of unsurpassed beauty, a light which some people call the Christ Light, or the Christ Presence. In the benediction of this light, the waves that ripple across the surface of Vohu Manah's sacred lake and surge through its body will be stilled into utter radiant calm. In either case,

you will be given the strength to perform the ceremony of
the violet flame given above.

Dispelling Negative Thoughts

When you sense that negative thoughts are lurking in your
vicinity and beginning to strike, call on Vohu Manah to seal
your crown centre, your unicorn's horn centre (at the top
of the forehead in the middle), your third eye (the chakra
situated in the middle of the brow ridge), the hollow of the
throat, the heart centre and the solar plexus centre with the
symbol of the bright silver-white equilateral cross within
a ring of pure light. Chant Vohu Manah's name quietly, or
silently within yourself if circumstances make it difficult to
speak aloud. You will feel the throng disperse and be able to
steer a positive course through the danger.

The Ship of Blessing

You can send out a thought-ship packed with provisions
of love and support to anyone or anywhere you feel there
is need, or simply as a gift of love. Spend some moments
visualizing a golden galleon with silver sails ready to begin
its voyage. See the cargo being brought aboard by angels,
who deposit it from their own essence. Summon the angels
individually (again, there is no need to worry about calling
on named angels if you prefer not to – simply enunciating
the quality you desire for your ship's cargo in association
with its angel is sufficient). For instance, you might call
on the angels of tranquillity, the angels of healing and
good health, the angels of blessed abundance, the angels
of energy, strength and motivation, the angels of restful
sleep, the angels of inspiration, the angels of harmonious
relationships, the angels of positive and loving discipline if

a friend with children is having a hard time, the angels of blessed opportunity, the angels of protection, the angels of replenishment, the angels of beauty, the angels of joy, etc, etc. Be as creative and wide-ranging as you like.

There are just three stipulations to bear in mind. The first is never to send the Ship of Blessing as an expression of judgment or interference: for instance, if you think that someone doesn't properly clean up their house, don't send them angels of hygiene and fastidiousness! The ship must always be a free gift from the heart, sent with the sole hope that its gifts will make its recipient feel better and happier and able to find more meaning and joy in life. It is important to send out healing ships, not corrective ships!

The second is to deck out the ship with flowers that are special to the person involved. If you know of no preference, roses are always a good option. Send forth the ship festooned in fragrant flowers, with a clear directive to its captain (who is Vohu Manah) as to where it is bound. This is accomplished simply by speaking the recipient's name three times and visualizing them in positive mode, relaxed and happy, as vividly as you can. Dedicate the flowers to the angels and to the person (or animal, natural object or situation) you are seeking to help.

The final stipulation is, via an act of visualization and intention, to send forth the ship under the sign and by the power of the six-pointed star, requesting that Michael and Gabriel accompany it to its destination. By doing this, you ensure that spiritual law is not broken in any way, because any gift within the ship that the recipient does not wish to receive will be withdrawn. It may even be their free-will choice to turn away the entire vessel. You will know if this happens. You can always send the ship out to them again, this time with gifts from the angels of self-worth firmly aboard. But if it is the recipient's wish still to decline your gift, their free-will choice is paramount and must at all times and all costs be respected.

The following chapter deals with the helpmeets and hand-maidens of Vohu Manah, with whom it is helpful to form a connection so that Vohu Manah's aid can be administered to its full potential. It comprises an extension of the rites of Vohu Manah via linkage with other Ka angels.

Chapter Seventeen
VOHU MANAH'S HELPMEETS AND HANDMAIDENS

Liromar and Consonia

The two handmaidens of Vohu Manah are Consonia and Liromar, who are likewise aided by Peta Rose and an angel whom I can only name Frankincense, although I would guess that the appellation is a working one designed to help us to understand her qualities rather than the ultimate invocation of her individual essence.

Consonia, Liromar and Peta Rose are three of a group of twelve angels to whom the American artist Mary Johanna gave form through her paintings.[3] The angels requested the opportunity of filling such appropriate receptacles with the fluidity, magic and beauty of their intrinsic being, and so it is possible actually to view these angels, which is a very powerful experience.

The third helpmeet of Vohu Manah is your own guardian angel. We can call on our guardian angel via a very simple ceremony, which involves lighting a white candle (this can always be envisioned if you cannot easily procure candles, or if there is a fire risk) at noon or at one of the other magical hours (3, 6, 9, 12). Ask your

---

3 The book containing the angel paintings is *The Angel of the Rays* by Mary Johanna, Oughten House Publications, Livermore, California, 1997, and can be purchased via the Internet.

guardian angel to alert you as soon as negative thoughts take over. It is surprising how unaware we can be of such marauders until they have cornered us into full-powered negative mode.

As always with the angels, it is important to make your petition very clear. You might say something such as:

> My guardian angel, please alert me as soon as
>   negative
> thoughts and feelings begin to encroach on me.
> Sound a call to remind me of my Pendragon
>   essence,
> and that Vohu Manah and the angels of heaven
>   stand
> ready to lift me up into its glorious light.

Make your request three times, thank the angel, and blow out the candle. Thereafter, you will feel a gentle nudge whenever negativity begins to gather its forces. It will be subtle, but unmistakable. As in all dealing with the angels, your free-will choice is paramount, and there will be no pressure or coercion in your guardian angel's approach. But, due to your angel's early warning system, the opportunity will unfailingly present itself to root out negativity in its initial stages each time it strikes. The more you take heed of your angel's warning, the clearer, more definite and precise will its warnings become.

Negative thoughts arise from negative feelings, and it is these we must address in our work with Vohu Manah. We can attune to Vohu Manah's helpmeets and other Ka angels according to our personal sources of difficulty. The conditions addressed below sound severe, but we will all encounter a number of them to some degree throughout our lives. Consonia and Liromar will help in each case. Their healing administrations are aided and consolidated by Peta Rose and Frankincense, and blessed by Yahriel, healer of hidden wounds.

The idea is to create a healing circle of angels with whom to work and on whom to call so that blocks and barriers may be removed from your path of progress with Vohu Manah. You will be calling on Ka angels in the main, so it is worth remembering that their methods of shifting obstruction are dynamic and sometimes awe-inspiring. Remember also the magic that dwells in the names of the angels; and in language itself if you prefer not to use names but would rather summon the angel simply via its qualities.

Calling the Healing Angels

Before you begin, ask Archangels Michael and Shekinah to protect you throughout your angel ceremony and throughout the day. Thank them.

Sit quietly in the early morning and invoke the circle of angels appropriate to your need (see Chapter 18) by repeating their names and/or their qualities in a gentle rhythmic chant. (Write their names and qualities down for easy reference during this process.)

Do your best to realize the presence of each one as it responds to your call.

Know that the angels are taking their positions in a complete circle around you, which enfolds and protects you.

As you chant, put out a silent request to them that they alert you to the angel, or angels, who will be able to help you most powerfully on that particular day according to your deepest needs and vulnerabilities.

Let your voice softly fall away into silence, and allow the angel or angels best suited to meet your need to come forward. You will feel an instinctive knowing. If this fails to happen, resume your chanting until you sense a gentle rush of energy as a certain name is sounded. Once this has happened, repeat the circuit of names twice more.

Further angels may present themselves, or they may remain quiet so that you know you will be working with a single angelic presence for the remainder of the day. It may even be that an entirely new and original angelic name reveals itself to you, or an angel not identified amongst the Ka angels. The ways of angels are diverse and mysterious, so always go with what you receive.

Ask the circle of angels to be with you throughout the day, and make a pact with the angels who have stepped forward to offer their specific aid that you will listen and respond to their guidance. Ask them to help you to do this.

As the day passes, find a moment as often as you can to chant the name or names of your specified angels, either silently or aloud (the merest whisper will suffice). They will give you pointers, challenges and promptings, which will lead you on a journey of self-discovery and innovation that you will recognize as your road to freedom from old constraints. Their counselling will come as a gentle, wise, lucid but non-insistent inner voice. Take heed of your angels. Every time you obey their prompting, their next directive will become clearer and more concise.

In the evening, sit quietly and call on Liromar and Consonia. Liromar will come from the eternal heart of Goddess on the green ray. She will put you in touch with your feelings and work her soft, surging tidal magic so that the great emotional charge within you is either stimulated or quietened according to your need and flows harmoniously throughout all the dimensions of your being.

Consonia, angel of the violet ray, of dreams and the bright half moon, will help you to deal with your shadow self. Buried trauma and heartbreak, guilt and blame, broken dreams, fragmented hopes, self-hatred, soul-disfigurements, a record of the times we turned away from the light – all is hidden in our subconscious. It is like a well shaft that must be cleared in order to reach the purity of the starlit water below. Consonia shows us how, and will merge with our guardian angel to offer every care and protection throughout this difficult but vitally necessary process. Consonia gives you her love and strength so that you may take a leap into the darkness, hand in hand with her angelic presence.

Liromar will bring you the sweet healing balm of the angel called Frankincense, who will enter into and heal your soul. Consonia will bring you the loveliness and gentleness of Peta Rose, who bears to us the rose fragrance of true self-nurture and self-love (not selfishness or egotism) so that we are brought gently into angelic harmony with neglected, rejected and suffering aspects of ourselves.

Spend time with Liromar and Frankincense, Consonia and Peta Rose, so that they are able to do the work of healing, soothing and integration that you need. Imagine their colours, which are, respectively, green, amethyst, violet and rose. Strangely enough, these angels are best summoned by song; not a jingle or a ditty, but a slow, musical singing of their names that dwells on each one. Try it and see where the melodies take you!

You will find that your heart opens to receive the blessing and the presence of these angels through the music that you create with your singing voice. (Don't worry if you are not musical – the angels will hear your notes in idealized mode!)

Draw your time with these four angels to a close by asking the angel Yahriel, healer of hidden wounds, to shed her light over you and your ceremony as a special benediction. Thank the angels.

Alovar

After each healing session with the four angels of the colours of the heart (Liromar, Frankincense, Consonia and Peta Rose), it is most important to conclude the day's entire angelic ceremony by calling on the fourth helpmeet of Vohu Manah, Alovar, whose colour is a soft, light, heavenly blue shot through with sparkling silver. He appears in folklore as the 'Knight Smitten by Love'. He represents perfect heart-wisdom when it comes forth as the deepest mystery from the feminine principle and is accepted and revered by the masculine principle rather than rejected by it. It is Alovar's task to convey this exquisite fount of heart-wisdom to waking consciousness. He awakens cellular memories, which hold within them the treasure store of the knowledge and wisdom of the entire panorama of our past lives. He does this as an act of integration between the psyche and the heart, for within the heart dwells the higher mind essence that connects us to God. When this is achieved, Vohu Manah's work is done.

Our conception and understanding of Alovar has again been conveyed to human consciousness via Mary Johanna's paintings and words. You might make your request to him by saying: 'Alovar, set the fountain of ineffable light springing in my heart. Let me express the flow of its love, truth and beauty in my inner and outer life. Thank you, angel of the silvery light blue ray.'

Chapter Eighteen
APPLYING KA ANGEL REMEDIES TO INDIVIDUAL PROBLEMS

It is worth once again contemplating the fact that in calling on the Ka Angels we are summoning an angelic force that might slap us around the face a little, in the nicest possible way! All contact with the angels is good and is to be highly recommended for our individual and collective growth, healing and reassurance. It is always a privilege and an honour to work with the angels. Nevertheless, when we consciously and specifically call on the Ka angels we are invoking the forces of spiritual alchemy in a way that declares we are ready to be challenged.

There is no need to worry, as the appropriate series of challenges will unfailingly be offered to us via our free-will choice, never by force. But the challenges will definitely come, and will wait to be taken up. It is important to be aware of this as we begin to interact with the Ka angels. As we work with them, we aspire toward ever-increasing harmony and attunement to Vohu Manah, the great angel of Good Thought. This is where our power to do magic resides – in the almost wholly unrecognized power of our thoughts and our imaginal configurations.

Within the mystic name of Vohu Manah lies the word 'human'. The rabbit language is confirming that our goal is to be 'fully human'. To be 'fully human' is indeed to become 'superhuman' in terms of our present-day understanding of what being human is. What it really is, and can be, is beyond our comprehension, even for those who work with angels. Yet, as we so work, we will catch glimpses, intimations, of what it truly means to be 'fully human'; and these flashing glimpses will give us joy and aspiration that will reach far beyond any mere material goal.

You can use the following suggestions to apply Ka angel remedies to individual problems, both for yourself and others, although it is important to seek permission first before invoking healing on another's behalf, except in a very general sense. If it is impossible to seek such permission, attune in meditation to the higher self of the person or group concerned and ask their guardian angel to guide you.

The previous chapter gives precise instructions on how to create the healing circle of angels and invoke their ministrations. Please study it carefully before working with the angelic healing circles.

DEPRESSION

Circle of angels:

Barbelo, Purveyor of Wisdom

Barbelo gently clears the heavy grey depressive mists that obscure the inner sun.

Camaysar, Angel of the Marriage of Contraries

Camaysar harmonizes and restores broken rhythm to areas of the psyche choked and gridlocked by conflict.

Chalchiuhtlicue, the Purifier

Chalchiuhtlicue's powerful force of purity and vitality throws off depression.

Charoum, Angel of Silence

Charoum dismantles the illusion of the dead, false silence

depression creates and brings the blessing of the healing, regenerative and sacred silence that is embedded like a jewel within the depths of every soul.

Consonia, Mistress of the Subconscious

Consonia shines a clear light on areas of difficulty and darkness whose need for resolution are the cause of the depression.

Eleleth, the Brightener

Eleleth brings a blaze of spiritual gold to oust depression.

Jophiel, Angel of Emancipation

Jophiel looses depressive bonds.

Liromar, Angel of Emotional Healing

Liromar brings the ease of free flow to feelings so that we can healthily access their energy instead of being choked and swamped by them.

Maion, Angel of Self-Discipline

Maion restores the peace and empowerment of self-discipline which depression drains away.

Melchior, Angel of Non-Judgment

Melchior, whose human expression found its focus in one of the three Magi or Wise Men (emissaries of Oannes/Enki or John), teaches us the art of non-judgmentalism, which is an essential component of love. This is also important in our view of ourselves. We need to assess ourselves, but never to judge or condemn, which leads to self-hatred and loathing and consequent despair. If this is a pitfall, perhaps even unrecognized, Melchior, the Wise Man bearing his gift to our Christ essence or our Pendragon self, will show us how to overcome it.

Peta Rose, Angel of Self-Worth

All people suffering from depression need to work closely with Peta Rose, who holds balm in her hands for the heart and for the weary and fainting earthly self.

Pyrhea, Angel of the Primal Force

If you are depressed, you need the energy charge of this angel; however, ask your guardian angel to mediate between you and Pyrhea, as her gifts need to be received safely.

Shemael, Angel of Gratitude

Depression is such a sickening energy that it takes away the sweetness and heart-opening of gratitude; Shemael restores this to us.

Tabris, Angel of Free Will

Our will power is obstructed in depression; Tabris calls back its vital force.

Vwyamus, Angel of Cleansing

Vwyamus purifies etheric mucus, and is an essential help-meet when depression strikes.

Yahriel, Healer of Hidden Wounds

Yahriel seeks out what we have denied and hidden, and brings forth a springing fountain of kindness, acknowledgement, mercy and healing to make hidden wounds whole.

Zadkiel, Angel of Ascension

Zadkiel lifts us above the misery of our depression and away from all the grasping hands and clamorous claims of our earthly nature and delivers our perception into the peace of the spiritual realm.

Zeruel, Angel of Strength

Depression has a deeply parasitic nature, and feeds on our strength and everything that comprises our vital force. Zeruel not only restores our flagging strength, but charges it with the dynamism to win triumphant freedom from the clutches of depression.

The angels say:

> It is in the depths of depression and lethargy that you can help most. You are closest to the forces that oppress humankind at such times. Will you dare to shine angelic light and the light in your own heart directly into these dark dominions? Not only will you throw off their tyranny for yourselves, but for the whole planet. It is among the most difficult, daring, courageous work we know. It astounds the dark forces. They are thrown into confusion, they fall back, they lose their grip. Your keynote must always be love. Raise your banner in the name of your inner flame, your Pendragon essence, the light that Christs you. Will you do this for us, beloved children of earth, so that, through you, we may enter with healing and glory into the deepest darkness of your domain for its healing?

ADDICTION

Circle of angels:

Baglis, Angel of Temperance

Baglis will stand at our back and strengthen our spine so that we don't buckle when the full force of the addiction we are seeking to overcome strikes hardest. He makes steadfast our will so that our decisions cannot be overturned. He imparts emotional balance and the peace and dignity of adhering to moderation.

Barbelo, Purveyor of Wisdom

Barbelo will offer kind counsel, in cases of addiction, that speaks to our depths, where the need for balance and a holistic expression of life resides; thus addiction begins to lose its grip.

Colopatiron, He Who Unlocks Prison Doors

The mighty Colopatiron, who released the biblical Peter from prison, turns the key, allows the door to your prison of addiction to open gently, and stretches out a reassuring hand so that you will not be afraid to leave.

Consonia, Mistress of the Subconscious

Work with Consonia if you suffer from addiction; as ever, she will root out the cause, which may perhaps be a need or a vulnerability you have never realized or addressed. She will show you your dark side, your shadow self; but she will demonstrate to you infallibly that it is your inner spiritual being of light – your Pendragon self – who is in charge, and whose gift and power it is to lift your shadow self gently into the healing light of the higher realms.

Frankincense, Sweetener of Sorrows

Frankincense will soften and ease the grief at the core of your addiction into a beautiful sorrow that can be expressed in tears, in art, in an unburdening of your heart, or by stepping through the door that its framework has created into higher consciousness. Sometimes, people hear notes of birdsong in the experience of this sorrow – sweet, fluting notes of deep warbling poignancy and pathos. Frankincense takes away all the ugliness and squalor of misery and transmutes it into a profound and beautiful emotional flow of sorrow.

Listen to music that expresses your sorrow when you call on Frankincense. She will lift you into its creative heart, so that your own is attuned to the wonderful compassion and healing of God's heart.

Gavreel, the Peace-maker

When you are addicted, you have given away your power to a vampiric force that imposes a distressing sado masochistic interaction upon you. The soul feels the humiliation and slavery as a deep sense of loss, almost as its own divinity lost or chained, and responds with sadness, anger, even desperation. To retrieve your authority and your dignity, you will need to make peace with yourself and the aspects of that self that you have denied or ignored. Gavreel brings you deep peace … deep peace of the running wave to you, deep peace of the shining stars to you, deep peace of the quiet earth to you … Gavreel makes peace, as if on a softly singing silver loom, and teaches you how to keep that spiritual device working and giving forth deep within yourself.

Liromar, Angel of Emotional Healing

Liromar from the sea will rise up in the hush and fall of the waves within the psyche, and carry you to the heart of things for your healing and release.

Maion, Angel of Self-Discipline

Maion waits to serve you and strengthen your resolve. He works with Baglis.

Melchior, Angel of Non-Judgment

Melchior will teach you to nurture yourself, and to accept gifts that acknowledge your worth and your courage.

Michael, Angel of Courage, Self-Empowerment and Protection

Michael imparts the qualities listed above in unstinting measure. When calling on him, you may even see the elemental entity that drives your addiction withering and wilting before the onslaught of his glorious light, which is the light of all guardianship and which is so akin to the light of the Christos. It may seem like a being of mist, becoming thinner and thinner until it loses all substantiality, even that of pure illusion.

Peta Rose, Angel of Self-Worth

Peta Rose, affirming and insisting on your sense of self-worth, will help you to overcome the violence and punishment you are imposing on yourself via your addiction. She will show you the difference between false and true love, false and true comfort and consolation. She will show you how to give yourself the nurturing, loving acceptance and healing that you need to become well again.

Rampel, Angel of Steadfastness and Resolution

In the case of healing addiction, Rampel works with Baglis. Rampel is the angel over mountains, and is ancient, steadfast and wise. He stands four-square and rooted, mighty and immoveable, however irresistible a force your addiction attempts to assume. Nothing can get past him. Rest in the peace and security of the unfailing sanctuary he offers.

Valoel, Angel of Peace

Seek the presence of Valoel to soothe the troubled waters of the soul. Enter into her beautiful light; meld with her so that, even while you perform the duties of every day, you walk in her bright hallows.

Var Bahram, Angel of Victory

Anyone struggling with addiction needs the aid and support of this glorious angel. Feel yourself enclosed in his mighty wings and claim the victory that is truly yours. Var Bahram says, 'The battle is worth the fight, for you will win!'

The Virtues, Angels of Transformation

The process of overcoming addiction is greatly aided by the Virtues. Some people speak of the Virtues as wondrous lights of exquisite and ever-changing colour that play over the area of the chakras. Others have spoken of smiling, dis-embodied faces that radiate love whose light is like that of a mountain on fire with supernal glory. They bring grace and valour to the soul, and a heavenly atmosphere, which initiates miracles and transformation. Let the Virtues surround you, and absorb their magical clemency.

Yahriel, Healer of Hidden Wounds

It is of great benefit, as always where vulnerability and the emotions are concerned, to call on gentle Yahriel in cases of addiction. However, we are working with the Ka angels in this context, so, although Yahriel will bestow her sweetness and kindness in locating hidden wounds, she will also expect her invocants to take motivated action in dealing with them.

The angels say:

If you are masculine, think of your Third Eye, located above and between your eyes on the brow ridge above your nose. Think of the physical eye to the left and the right below it. Now see the shape that the three eyes make as an emerald green pyramid, star-bright and pure. Let it fill with light from the highest angelic realms, which are connected to your heart. It is the Abode of Joy.

If you are feminine, you will be aware of the pyramid jewel your three eyes make together. Yet think also of the divine crucible that is your womb. It is always there, no matter what might have befallen the physical vehicle. You will feel a very tender light of love flowing from your heart and shining into the secret depths of that crucible. Let the special quality of that love flow often into your womb. Your own sensitivity will tell you that it is antiphonal. There is magic of the highest order in it. The emerald pyramid of sacred seeing has its source here, for in the uterus, the utterer of the Divine Word, is the secret of Creation and of God.

Fill yourself often with this divine magic dwelling in the Abode of Joy, in the sacred uterus. It will release you from the ruffianly grip of the fiercest addiction, and open horizons beyond your present conception.

TRAUMATIC MEMORIES

Circle of angels:

Angels of Mercy

The Angels of Mercy are traditionally known as Michael, Gabriel and Zadkiel. They will surround you with the peace and gentleness of the healing you need when you embark on the task of laying bad memories to rest.

Baglis, Angel of Temperance

If your distress caused by traumatic memory is tempestuous, if your emotions are charging and panic escalates, you need the consoling hand of Baglis on your brow to bring you the calm control of temperance.

Chalchiuhtlicue, the Purifier

Chalchiuhtlicue will help to wash away the psychological pathology generated by painful memories. She surges through the dank subterranean airlessness of the inner dungeons where they reside and brings quickening, purity and sunshine to these paralysed areas. She lifts us away from being stuck in a groove and moves traumatized energy on. She prepares the ground for new seeds.

Chamuel, Angel of Kindly Justice

It is almost inevitable that you will need to make an act of forgiveness if you have traumatic memories, even if you only need to forgive the circumstances that plunged you into them (such as a blameless car crash, for instance). Chamuel will help to calm you and to see things in quiet and undramatic perspective. She fortifies you against dread and psychological suffering, and provides the first step toward opening the heart in forgiveness.

Colopatiron, He Who Unlocks Prison Doors

Colopatiron has the power to release the psyche from the oppressive lock-up imposed by bad memories. Feel the tension easing, the vortex stilling, and the healing presence of Colopatiron granting you release. But he does not only do this.

He destroys the prison behind you as you make your bid for freedom. Once you have truly linked hands and destiny with Colopatiron, its doors can never close on you again.

Consonia, Mistress of the Subconscious

Consonia will work with Chalchiuhtlicue to release tightly lodged memories of pain, fear, horror or abuse. It is important to work closely with her in the case of traumatic memories, because she has special access to the individual subconscious.

She shows us methods of release that are specially attuned to our personal needs. She knows at which point the needle of our safety gauge will move to overload, and she will ensure that we never approach too close to that tip-over point. She prepares a place for us to rest and regroup after each stage of the labour of dealing with bad memories. She paces us. She works with the divine dynamic in the consciousness of God that bids us lie down in green pastures for the restoration of the soul.

Elemiah, Angel of Inner Journeying

Beyond the misery and turmoil of bad memories lies the path to transformation.

Something beautiful and lyrical will enter your soul as you holistically process your experiences. Elemiah waits to guide you on your journey of release.

Frankincense, Sweetener of Sorrow

Frankincense will work with the Angels of Mercy to bring you release from your trauma. She says: 'Imagine your trauma as a red-hot zigzag, bright crimson in colour, against a glaring white background. Now see its angry heat become gentle warmth, slowly, slowly. Its colour has turned into a beautiful, glowing, shell-pink. See the pink zigzag shape transform into a figure of eight with a gentle continuous flow. Gradually, the figure of eight becomes circular until it turns into a sweet wild rose, briar-pink, emitting wondrous fragrance. The background softly mists over with green sunlit foliage. The heart of the rose is golden. All is well.'

Hahaiah, Angel of Reconciliation

Hahaiah harmonizes with the angel of peace to bring reconciliation to the experience of your trauma and the circumstances that surround it.

Liromar, Angel of Emotional Healing

Liromar and Consonia join forces to help us confront and work through blockages and dangerous areas. Liromar also assists Chalchiuhtlicue in supplanting the power of the traumatic-memory whirlpool with a surging wave of new energy bearing new tidings.

The power of the traumatic-memory whirlpool is sinister and brutal. It pulls us into the depths of its greatest force against our strongest will and re-enacts through us the anguish of the trauma. Consonia, Liromar and Chalchiuhtlicue form a pyramidal force to deliver us from this torture chamber.

Michael, Angel of Courage, Self-Empowerment and Protection

Michael will bring you the protection, strength and resolve you need to overcome the serpent-strength of the fear or hopelessness caused by traumatic memories.

Peta Rose, Angel of Self-Worth

Peta Rose appears to help you, in her true form of an angelic rose, wild and pink as a flame-flushed sunrise. As you see, she is working with Frankincense to bring you healing balm. She enfolds you in a robe of self-acceptance and self-nurture, and takes all your suffering into the heart of the rose of her being to allow the burden of painful vibration to dissolve into peace.

Phanuel, Angel of Forgiveness

Phanuel, also the angel of hope and contrition, helps us to open our heart in forgiveness of others and of ourselves.

Tabris, Angel of Free Will

The angels teach us to think of our free will, not so much as a force of wandering caprice that does as it pleases, but as the power of free choice.

Therefore, whatever might descend upon us, we can choose our responses. This is extremely difficult to realize in the case of trauma or pain, when a brutal ineluctability seems to inform our reactions. Yet there is still that scarcely discernible leeway, obscured, difficult to place, but nonetheless in existence, where we can impose our free-will choice. When we are ready, Tabris takes us to that concealed place and gives us the mastery to choose to let go. Healing is necessary first, and resolution of the darkness that the trauma has invoked.

Valoel, Angel of Peace

Peace-blessed Valoel, descending on quiet wings, lifts the soul into stillness and sanctuary. Take the time often to align your heartbeat with his. He will connect you ever more deeply and powerfully to that inner sanctuary of perfect peace, where all is good, all is well, and the illusions of dread, pain, suffering and cruelty lose their potency. Whenever fearful memories are sparked off, you will recognize each time that their tyranny and their power of fascination are fading.

Yahriel, Healer of Hidden Wounds

Once again, Yahriel stands by to pour her balm onto the anguished rawness of what hides in the darkness of our subconscious.

The angels say:

> Remember our brother Alovar, Keyholder to the Treasury. He comes forward with a gift in his hands once you have jumped the hurdle of unresolved and distressing memories, and indeed any deep wounding. It is a key. You have arrived at a threshold. He is there to take you within and show you the treasures that have been waiting for you and that you may now claim. Brave soul!
>
> The angels honour you for what you chose to endure, so that you might come to this storehouse and win the riches secreted within.

CONFLICTED ASPECTS OF PERSONALITY

Circle of angels:

Ambriel, Angel of Reflections

Ambriel, angel of opposites and twinned reflections, facilitates clear communication between dissonant aspects of the self, and opens up a channel so that interior confusion and colliding energies can be clarified and harmonized.

Balthiel, Thwarter of Jealousy

Feelings of jealousy and resentment can cause conflicted aspects of personality. If this is an underlying problem, Balthiel can help by revealing the condition and bringing healing light to aggrieved feelings. His bold but compassionate influence allows us to be ourselves, without defiance or confrontation and, most importantly, free from feelings of guilt, shame or apology. When this harmony is taken deep into the soul, the spectre of jealousy flees.

Barbelo, Purveyor of Wisdom

Barbelo will bless you with her healing guidance when you feel out of harmony with yourself, and as if warring factions within constrict you or are preventing you from moving forward.

Camaysar, Angel of the Marriage of Contraries

When we feel conflicting pushes and pulls within that generally result in rooting us to the spot in our life situations, we can bring warmth and life to our frozen predicament by working with the wisdom and magic of Camaysar.

Colopatiron, He Who Unlocks Prison Doors

Colopatiron releases us from the prison of stuck energy within the personality.

If you have every intention of following a plan, but repeatedly fail to do so, or if your ideas never catch fire in the outer world, Colopatiron will show you how to release yourself from your shackles and move on.

Consonia, Mistress of the Subconscious

Consonia tracks a path through the wilderness of the subconscious, and beckons us on.

As always, she will bring up issues from murky depths, and show us therapeutic ways to tackle them.

Eleleth, the Brightener

Eleleth, a mighty power among angels, encompasses and balances ice and fire, and what those principles mean in the subtle worlds of the collective psyche. He brightens and blesses every situation in which humans call on him. He is the higher power overlighting Hahaiah.

Gavreel, the Peace-Maker

Gavreel operates with Ambriel, Camaysar, Eleleth and Hahaiah to bring what is conflicted within into the realm of unassailable peace.

Hahaiah, Angel of Reconciliation

Merciful Hahaiah works with her guiding light, Eleleth, to reconcile opposing dynamics within the psyche.

Liromar, Angel of Emotional Healing

Allow Liromar of the sea to loosen, ease and dissolve psychological blockages and embattled, locked energies.

Her rise and fall, the soft boom of her hushing cadence, will lull and cradle your dissonant energetic fields and their broken rhythm until their forces become a peaceful, flowing confluence of resolved energies.

Maion, Angel of Self-Discipline

Maion will bring you the peace and focus of intrinsic discipline in dealing with your problem.

Omniel, Angel of Unity

Working with Camaysar, Eleleth, Gavreel, Hahaiah and Ambriel, Omniel, enfolding angel of one-pointed unity, strikes the final blow, so to speak, or, to express it more angelically, delivers the final healing incantation, which pulls our disparate parts back together into a seamless whole.

Peta Rose, Angel of Self-Worth

The gift of Peta Rose is a holistic sense of self-worth and self-love, essential for all healing at deep inner levels.

Yahriel, Healer of Hidden Wounds

Yahriel's balm is always particularly needed in cases of an afflicted psyche.

The powerful angels with which to attune when working to overcome conflicted aspects within the personality are Camaysar, Eleleth, Gavreel and Hahaiah (*see* Chapter Four) and also Ambriel and Omniel. The other angels listed play their part, of course, and are also important.

The angels say:

Work with our brethren listed above when you are labouring to integrate your soul forces, but also with golden Mithra. Remember the feminine aspect of Mithra in your apperception of this great angelic presence. His holy rites will make whole the dislocated soul.

GRIEF

Circle of angels:

Charoum, Angel of Silence

Within the silence lies the jewel that will light your way. Withdraw from the jangling pettiness of the world, and allow Charoum to gift you with the healing of silence.

Colopatiron, He Who Unlocks Prison Doors

Grief is a dungeon. It can seem impossible to continue with life, as though we would have to live it enclosed in grief's terrible subterranean prison. Colopatiron comes to ease our way out of our dark incarceration and takes us into the soft light of sorrow, where the heart, still mourning, can breathe again and begin to perceive the beauty in its pain.

Consonia, Mistress of the Subconscious

Consonia will help us to tackle any danger-area in the subconscious that might exacerbate the anger and horror in grief and turn it toward madness. She will also monitor the depths of grief so that it does not become trapped as large areas of paralysis and pathology within the psyche.

Eleleth, the Brightener

In grief, we need the mighty positive force of this angel, and his promise of transformation of darkness into light.

Elemiah, Angel of Inner Journeying

Elemiah will take us on a journey of expansion of the soul which is the gift of grief. Elemiah ensures that it is not a harsh and bitter journey.

Frankincense, Sweetener of Sorrows

Frankincense blesses the ministrations of Gavreel, and brings a gentle release into a beautiful sorrow from the ravages of grief.

Gavreel, the Peace-Maker

Anger is almost always a component of grief. Gavreel brings peace and tenderness to raw and angry feelings.

Haamiah, Angel of Truth

We need the angel of truth to help us to see clearly when we are plunged into grief. No situation is hopeless, and no goodbye is forever. Haamiah will assist us in realizing the deep truth of goodness and mercy that lies behind our loss or disappointment. Even when ugly and brutal things happen because of the ignorance of humanity, this spirit of goodness and mercy never dies.

Hahaiah, Angel of Reconciliation

Hahaiah works with Gavreel and Haamiah to bring us into the peace of reconciliation with our fate. Taking this gentle, angelic way, we do not lose power in the process of becoming reconciled, but gain it.

Liromar, Angel of Emotional Healing

Liromar understands the devastation of grief and heartbreak. She will connect us with our loved one, if we are bereaved, or take us into gardens of remembrance if we have lost touch with the person we were before the devastation struck.

Maion, Angel of Self-Discipline

It is almost inevitable that grief will swamp us with self-pity at some point during our experience of it. Self-pity can weigh very heavily on the soul and prevent it from finding its feet. Maion can be relied upon to help us to recognize self-pity when it sets in and to steer us firmly away from it for the sake of our own healing.

Melchior, Angel of Non-Judgment

It is essential to work with Melchior when grief strikes, so that we refrain from judging ourselves, life, and others and thus binding ourselves into the fastnesses of our grief.

Shemael, Angel of Gratitude

In the case of grief, Shemael works with Maion to help to restore our sense of gratitude for our blessings. Grief can transform our capacity for gratitude into a sweetly poignant healing force, like a replenishing spring.

The Virgin of Light, Lamp-Bearer Sublime

The Virgin of Light shines an effulgent beam of wisdom into the grieving soul, reconnecting it with its intuition and allowing it to see the greater and nobler truth manifesting behind the apparently meaningless and brutal earthly circumstances surrounding the cause of its grief.

Zeruel, Angel of Strength

We come to Zeruel when we are worn out and worn down with the battering and punishments of life. Grief undermines and erodes, sometimes even blasting our strength on every level. Zeruel stands by to revive, re-arm and re-shoe us, so that we can continue along our designated path.

HOPELESSNESS

Circle of angels:

The serving circle is the same as that for DEPRESSION (*see* pages 163–66), with the addition of:

Var Bahram, Angel of Victory

Var Bahram reminds the soul suffering from hopelessness that the whole of creation was designed specifically so that we might achieve victory in our endeavours. Earth is a school for souls created by God, and it is inconceivable that such a school should set up its pupils for failure! Within every soul is the seed of the Divine, and the essence of the Divine contains within it everything the soul needs to achieve victory. If we do not win according to earthly standards, we may be sure that the opportunity is offering itself for a much more important victory in soul-forging, which is why we are here. Victory is our sure and certain hope as Children of Light, as children of God. We are sons of the King, daughters of the Queen, and when our true desire is to achieve victory, we cannot fail. Var Bahram stands as surety of this revelation and unfailing promise.

Zuriel, the Enlightener

There is sometimes a tendency to be rather gleeful in pessimism. Life seems to confirm and reinforce the outcome of hopelessness, and there is a temptation to crow, as if our gloom and doom philosophy is revealed as wise and mighty. At such times we fall prey to what Mary Magdalene in her gospel calls Guileful Wisdom, the false wisdom beckoning us down a path of stupidity. What could we need more at such times than the influences of the angel Zuriel, 'curer of stupidity in man'? Once the pain and sorrow dwelling in the depths of hopelessness are healed, we have to oust the residue of stubbornness that allows it to persist.

OBSESSION

Circle of angels:

The circle of angels is the same as that for ADDICTION (*see* pages 166–70).

DESPERATION

Circle of angels:

The serving circle is the same as that for ADDICTION (*see* pages 166–70), with the addition of:

Eleleth, the Brightener

The mighty power of Eleleth, radiating glorious positivity and embracing polar opposites in a harmonious circle of unity, waits to serve us when we are cast into desperate circumstances or experience feelings of desperation. He shows us an ascending staircase out of our dilemma. We can ascend it entirely surrounded and supported by the warm presence of his irresistible light.

Hahaiah, Angel of Reconciliation

Allow Hahaiah to soothe terrible feelings of desperation with her power to reconcile your soul with what you cannot bear. Remember that her gift is not resignation, but reconciliation. When peace is made deep within the dimensions of what brings anger or anguish, then the way forward, leading out of the condition of entrapment, begins to appear.

The Virgin of Light, Lamp-Bearer Sublime

The Virgin of Light will enfold you in her radiance and reconnect you to your 'in-tuition', the wise teacher within. Desperation and urgency will be supplanted by a calm feeling of self-mastery and interior clarity as the sublime ray of the Virgin blesses your chakras and brings you to a state of inner knowing.

BODIES OF STAGNANT ENERGY WITHIN THE SUBCONSCIOUS MIND

These manifest as stuck energy, whereby you feel frozen in your expression of life.

If you find it difficult to put your will into action, in small matters as well as large; if things tend not to work out for you, if you feel generally tired and burdened and sense a slowness and heaviness restricting your mental and physical capacities, it is likely that bodies of stagnant energy are present within your psyche.

Circle of angels:

The serving circle is the same as that for DEPRESSION (*see* pages 163–66), with the addition of:

Pathiel, Opener of the Way

Pathiel, serene angel of the paths of destiny, waits to open the way for those who have lost direction in their soul. Beyond the obstruction, beyond the dead end, beyond the edge of the precipice, lies the angel-lit path that the flame of spirit dwelling within each of us has chosen in order to fulfil our life purpose. Pathiel floods it with clarifying radiance so that it appears like a wonder in the shifting and disappearing mists of our confusion; he ushers our faltering feet safely onto its bright forward-leading way.

The Virgin of Light, Lamp-Bearer Sublime

Sufferers from stagnant psychic energy need to enter into dialogue with these paralyzed bodies in the psyche and discover their source and the meaning of their manifestation. The Virgin of Light facilitates and smoothes this difficult process.

Zlar, Revealer of Wisdom

Lucent Zlar clarifies the knowledge that the Virgin reveals and conducts it from the delicacy of the subconscious to the concretion of the intellect, so that it may be fully realized on every level.

GUILT and SHAME

Circle of angels:

The serving circle is the same as that for TRAUMATIC

MEMORIES (*see* pages 171–75), with the addition of:

Maion, Angel of Self-Discipline

Guilt and shame can become addictive in the same way that self-harming or self-flagellation incorporate addictive and obsessive qualities. Maion halts the uncontrolled drive towards self-indulgence and helps us to recognize it even when it takes the form of inflicting punishment on the self.

Melchior, Angel of Non-Judgment

Melchior will gently lead you to understand that judging yourself with harshness and condemnation is as harmful, destructive and unfair as it is to sit in judgment on others. He will show you how to release yourself from your own judgement and from fear of the judgment of others.

Pedael, Angel of Deliverance

Pedael lifts us out of the agonizing cycle of guilt and shame. He teaches us how to supplant it with compassion.

DEEP-ROOTED SENSE OF INADEQUACY AND UNWORTHINESS

Circle of angels:

The serving circle is the same as that for ADDICTION (*see* pages 166–70), with the addition of:

Haniel, Angel of Confidence

Haniel surrounds us with a warm comforting glow and heals and stimulates our sense of self-assurance.

Pedael, Angel of Deliverance

Pedael delivers us from the oppression we inflict on ourselves. He works with Melchior and Rachmiel (see below) to loosen the chains of self-judgement with which we have shackled ourselves.

Phanuel, Angel of Forgiveness

When we have judged ourselves as unworthy and below

par, we need to forgive our earthly self for imposing a false and godless judgement that has done so much harm. Phanuel helps us to forgive the foolishness and destructiveness within that led to the expression of such 'guileful wisdom' (false and malignant wisdom), and to refrain from judging ourselves for falling into its trap!

Rachmiel, Angel of Compassion

Rachmiel sends forth an influence of compassion that melts away the knots and tangles and stony places in the soul. Kindly, life-giving rivers flow into barren valleys and forgotten dead lands within its dimensions.

SELF-LOATHING

Circle of angels:

The serving circle is the same as that for DEPRESSION and DEEP-ROOTED SENSE OF INADEQUACY AND UNWORTHINESS (*see* pages 166–70), with the addition of:

Azura, Angel of Tranquillity

Azura, who comes in on the exquisite azure blue ray and is one of the angels brought to our consciousness by Mary Johanna, heals anger and the raging need for destructiveness.

Anger is at the heart of self-loathing, and at the heart of anger dwells the need to transform this wayward energy into love. Peta Rose works with Azura to help a soul struggling with this crisis, knowing that in the same instant that you learn to love yourself, you learn to love all of humanity, and its divine source.

BLOCKAGES OF THE PSYCHE EMBEDDED IN PRESENT AND PAST-LIFE EXPERIENCES

Circle of angels:

The serving circle is the same as that for TRAUMATIC MEMORIES (*see* pages 171–75), with the addition of:

Melchior, Angel of Non-Judgement

Melchior waits to release us from strictures of past judgment imposed by ourselves, or judgments imposed by others that we have taken deep into ourselves.

Pedael, Angel of Deliverance

Pedael comes to us as an act of mercy when our forward path is blocked.

The Sword of Michael

Pedael works with Michael to cut us free from the past. The sword of Michael descends and sets us free. The sword does not cut away precious bonds of love, but only what constricts and chokes our path.

The Virgin of Light, Lamp-Bearer Sublime

In cases of past-life traumas and sorrows, or repressed memories, there is a deep need for the lamp of the Virgin of Light to cast its merciful rays over what lies hidden in the darkness.

REPRESSED OR MANIFESTING ANGER

Circle of angels:

The serving circle is the same as that for SELF-LOATHING (*see* opposite), with the addition of:

Sandalphon, Angel of the Earth

When anger catches you up into its tornado, discharge its energy into the earth. Point your fingers downward and let its elemental force rush from your hands and feet and forehead down into the good stable earth. Call on Sandalphon, the great angel of earth, to help you to do this so that no harm comes to you or the earth in the process.

POINTERS

Remember Alovar as you work through the problems you bring to the angels. **Alovar, Keyholder to the Treasury,** can gift you with what lies in your treasury once you have shifted your subconscious hindrances.

Remember **Shekinah, Angel of All-Embracing Love.** Her influence is with you from the outset as you work your way through your difficulties, and she waits to embrace you at the end of your labours. Without attunement to her, no final healing can take place. Accept her essence into your heart to be healed.

You are likely to find yourself working with quite a number of angels. There is no need to feel daunted, as a certain group, or even a single angel, will step forward to work with you. These angels are all you need to focus on at any one time. When your work with them is done, they will withdraw quietly, ready to serve you again whenever the need arises.

You may at this point believe that your endeavour is complete and your problem healed. If not, resume your practice of calling on the full circle of angels you initially invoked. Others will come forward to help you further.

If your problem is simpler than those listed, choose a Ka angel to help you by calling on the aid of **Eistibus, Angel of Divination.** Your stumbling block might be lack of focus, for instance. Eistibus may well point you in the direction of the ministrations of **Rampel, Angel of Steadfastness and Resolution.** Or if you suffer from aggressiveness, **Peta Rose** (for self-worth), **Shekinah** (for unconditional love),

Frankincense (for gentleness and sweetness) and a combination of the influences of **Gavreel** and **Valoel** (for peace) might be indicated. Your own intuition may serve you; if not, **Eistibus** will show the way.

Angelic communication is always simple, without any overload of the intellect; in fact, this prevents it. Angelic consciousness is profound, much more so than the levels of the intellect, and indeed it blesses and deepens the dimensions of the human intellect. But it does not work within its narrow restrictions and tensions. It is gentle, peaceful, and conveys a sense of ease.

The Ka angels with whom you work will give you tasks and present you with challenges. These are your therapy, so it is important not to ignore them. If you do, your contact with the angels will become less vital. To ensure that your inspiration is coming from the angels, just ask three times for this to be confirmed (not in succession unless unavoidable). When confirmation comes for the third time, and if your intuition (not your inclination) feels at peace, it is right to act.

Chapter Nineteen
THE FACELESS WOMAN

Among the very highest of the high within the ranks of the Zoroastrian angels stands Anahita, of brightest magnitude and unconscionable beauty. For me, she is the personification of the consciousness of Brigid, the feminine expression of the great Christ being, daughter–son of God, who stands at the pinnacle of creation, calling us on. For this reason, Brigid has been known from ancient times as the Shepherdess. And it is as the Shepherdess that this angelic sister of Brigid greets us now, for she has a message to impart and a way to illuminate that are vital to our understanding at this time.

Anahita has been called 'the immaculate one, genius of fertilizing water and of the fruitfulness of the earth'. She is associated with the great archangel Aramaiti, She of Holy Harmony, who has guardianship of all creative forces on earth. Anahita's essence is similarly the essence of the Sacred Feminine, of Goddess. Her association with fertilizing water and fruitfulness shows us that she is mistress of the forces of exalted sexuality. These forces are indeed part of her very essence, an expression of the dynamo of Divine Spirit, its veritable creative pulse. To fully understand and appreciate Anahita's mission at this time, and her leading role in the battle against the Faceless Woman, it is necessary to recapitulate very briefly the story of Enki and Enlil.

Enki and Enlil: A Summary

There seems to be strong (I believe, incontrovertible) evidence permeating history that there were two brothers, human beings so advanced that we would think of them today as 'superhuman', who came to this earth with a small number of their people to oversee the establishment of a younger, less advanced humanity (ourselves), which would be implanted in animal bodies. It was God's decree that this embryonic humanity should grow and progress via the strictures of densest matter until it reached the same status as that of the advanced humanity, which had overseen its instigation. The result would be a forward movement for all creation, because the physical domain – the one furthest from God – would thereby be brought into full operational harmony with God. The domain of matter would have been won by the forces of light, allowing them to surpass their present boundaries. It was a daring and innovative plan of cosmic proportions: a beautiful service to God that humanity was eager to undertake and, by the same token, a gift beyond measure from God to humanity.

One of these brothers was steadfastly attuned to the light of God, while the other lost his footing in the prevailing earthly conditions, eventually denouncing God and falling into darkness and evil. He became disgusted with physicality and regarded it as inferior and impure. He could not bear that his own kind (humanity), whom he saw as gods in charge of creation, should degrade itself by entering into the vile substance of matter. He decided that the whole idea of implanting human beings into animal bodies was evil, and that, as it had been decreed by a God perceived to have its source in the Feminine Principle, this God must be evil, and the true God an all-male God. The ill-willed brother stole his brother's right to kingship and set himself up as ruler, asserting male dominance and the wholesale degradation of women and the Sacred Feminine.

This ill-willed brother was determined to see earth's humanity fail, and the planet itself become so devastated that it would never again be able to support human life. Manipulation of confused and benighted humankind would be his lethal weapon.

The light-attuned brother who should have been king has worked tirelessly throughout millennia to thwart his brother's evil plans (both brothers being far beyond subjection to the physical cycles of birth and death that it is necessary for us to endure). He has been known throughout the ages as Enki, Oan, Thoth, Poimandres, Oannes and the John-Man, manifesting his essence within noble souls who served the cause of the light. such as Moses, Taliesin, John the Baptist, John the Beloved Disciple, Joseph of Arimathea, the seer Merlin and King Arthur among many, many others belonging to all traditions. He preceded the coming of the Christ (expressed on earth through Jesus and Mary Magdalene) to prepare the way. He was behind the materialization of the Fisher King, showing us the true agonized state of the Masculine Principle when his bride, the Feminine Principle, has been torn away from his heart and his genitals. The fused being, now split in two, remains in a state of bereavement and agony until the healing of conjoinment takes place.

Enki, the good brother, was the first Gentle Man, and instigated the idea of knights: Gentle and Noble Men who honoured the Sacred Feminine and regarded women as equals. He taught the arts of civilization to humanity. He was determined that we, the younger humanity that his people had brought to earth, should attain the same elevated status as the supremely developed humanity to which he belonged and over which he should rightfully be king. He, with his wife Nin-Khursag, initiated a temple whose knowledge passed to Zarathustra or Zoroaster, Enki's faithful servant.

Zarathustra cemented the teachings of light that comprised this temple into human consciousness, and out of them arose all the many doctrines that have sought to ennoble humanity. It is from Enki that we have our knowledge of angels.

Enki hid and protected a secret deep within his heart, a secret that Enlil (the cruel, tyrannical brother) and his forces were determined at all costs to deny and destroy.

The secret was that Mother God was the source of all, and that Father God, although her equal in every sense, came forth from her and was expressed by her. Wherever this secret was cherished, Enlil brought to bear his hideous manipulations with psychopathic strength and determination. A few of the historical instances of this (and they are legion) include the slaughter of the Templars and the Cathars, and the sudden and terrifying outbreaks of witch-burnings across Europe. In the case of the Cathars, who enshrined a partial knowledge and use of the Grail in their culture, their bodies were dug up years and even decades after their murder and savagely desecrated and destroyed as if, interestingly, it was intended that their very DNA should be eradicated.

We can think of Enki as the supreme master of the alchemical craft, which works with God to build higher human consciousness. This is the gold-bestowing magic that forges our souls through the hammer blows of physical life and purges us in the fire of physical experience. He was known as 'the manifestation of knowledge and the craftsman *par excellence*', who drove out all darkness that afflicted humankind and who worked with Mithra, the angel of glory known as the Son of Light, or what we might think of as the angelic aspect of Christ consciousness. Mithra, brightest angel within the embrace of Michael and Shekinah and in a sense their 'child', is associated with Enki because he was the great forger, the alchemist, the worker with the divine fires of God.

It was these divine fires – the unassailable Light – that Enki taught Zarathustra (called Ham in the Old Testament) to worship: the divine fire within that connects us to God and is God and which confirms us as beings of ultimate light – Pendragons, invested with the supreme gift of breathing forth those divine fires in our individual essence. Mithra is also the Daughter of Light, and this aspect of Mithra is most beautifully expressed in the angelic essence of Anahita.

Enki's followers were taught that when they looked upon the form of womanhood, they looked on God. The delight that they experienced was a joyful recognition of a profoundly spiritual truth – Enki's secret – and was expressed in a surge of heart-worship of the Sacred Feminine and Mother God. However, it was by no means the pornographic rush that is generally sought today.

Far from degrading a woman as an object of predation and the lust that precedes the desire to predate, this piercing of the heart by a woman's unveiled mystery lifted the percipient into an ascension of consciousness. They saw, not an enslaved plaything, but the deeper being of the woman and her connection to Mother God, which set alight their own connection. Perceiving her in this way was in itself a personal honouring of the Sacred Feminine, and a personal recognition, born from impersonal love, of the mystery of the woman perceived.

Some years ago, a Japanese man who calls himself the 'godfather of cannibals' fulfilled his fantasy by killing and eating a young woman upon whom he had fixed his sexual desire. A succession of unusual circumstances ensured that, although convicted of the crime, his time in detention was very short. He is currently a celebrity who enjoys a high-profile status and is invited to feature in pornographic films specifically because of what he did.

This situation seems to indicate that Enlil's plan that we should entirely lose sight of the Sacred Feminine and replace that exquisite percipience with the grossest degradation and wholesale sexual consumerism is working very well. There is no sense that this approach is an abomination. Despite the reality of the 'godfather of cannibals', pornography, which in its essence is concerned with degradation, sexual enslavement and the desire to predatorially devour, is seen as fashionable, inevitable and harmless. However, the teaching of the heart informs us that there are things, in a very literal and direct sense, which arise from pornography: astral life-forms that configure themselves into entities of a highly dangerous and sinister nature.

The first point to consider is the harm to women. Both collectively and individually, women are harmed by the bombardment of degrading lusts continually aimed at them and at the idea of them. Soft porn, which is inescapable, is anything but innocuous. It is a reminder, everywhere, all the time, like the slow drip of continuously-applied medication, that men should maintain a derisive attitude toward the Feminine Principle as an enslaved object to serve a base self-gratification, and a similarly continuous reminder to women that they should knuckle down and put up with it. A whole raft of condemnation is employed against them should they seek to step out of line, one aspect of which most commonly is that the dehumanizing of women in this way is an 'inevitable' and 'natural' expression of masculine sexuality. Also, that a woman who objects to her partner having remote sex with as many other women as he can, and to being, during coitus, nothing more than a kind of venue for the expression of such collected generic lusts for women, is somehow illiberal and narrow-minded.

From just the same controlling source arose the advice given to women of the past that their husbands were 'bound' to be unfaithful and that therefore they must just put up with the resultant heartbreak and humiliation and remember that 'women were born to pain.' Among many other degradations, the justification of the harem mentality (which boils down to the statement that 'one of me is equal to a limitless number of you'; a stance encouraged by a number of religions) thus continues unchallenged. And additionally, there are pragmatic points to consider. The rise in breast cancer since photographs of topless women were placed in daily papers and stacked on the top shelves of newsagents and other outlets has soared. It is not possible to alienate a part of womanhood from her soul and deeper being for purposes of abusive objectification and gross gratification without simultaneously creating such a hazard. The very fact that we support the status of a magazine called *Zoo* in our society, where women are likened to animals ranged behind bars for the lascivious visual devouring of male consumers, points to the degree to which we have allowed our minds and attitudes to become chained and controlled by sinister puppet-masters.

A woman who has exposed herself to the direct reception of collective visual lust (a lap-dancer, for instance), is seen when viewed astrally as hung with disturbing and sinister garments that explode and re-form with an energy which is threatening, squalid and extremely malignant. It is the very opposite of an expression of innocuous and harmless fun. Not only does it injure the individual herself, but the invidious energy discharged from dehumanizing sexual lust also directs itself to a great pool, like a whirlpool of horror and black intent, which operates unseen in the thought spheres.

From it arise elemental creatures of a sadistic and psychopathic nature, which are under the command of a certain lord or elemental king. He directs these creatures to enter into and manipulate those human beings where he can see a weakness. This weakness has become a moral weakness, but it is important to understand that the breach will initially have occurred because the individual concerned experienced severe suffering and abuse, either in this life or in a past incarnation. They are not just random human monsters. However, because of their susceptibility, their behaviour becomes monstrous in the extreme, and yet another woman is found mangled and murdered after having undergone sexual torture. Their bodies are often reported as being discovered on 'wasteland', which in itself is symbolic and telling.

There is worse to come. The degradation and gross objectification of the Sacred Feminine leads directly to the sexual abuse of children. There is a definite and undeniable link when this behaviour is viewed from the eyrie of spiritual vision. It is not possible to practise wholesale abuse of the Sacred Feminine without such imposed ignominy rebounding on the innocence and vulnerability of children. If the sanctity of the mother is dishonoured and despised for long enough, the violating principle begins to transfer itself to the status of the child. Unfortunately, it makes no difference that the majority of those who use soft porn would never sexualize or harm a child. They simply help to forge a link that is used by others: behaviour, according to the deeper laws of life, which is both inevitable and ineluctable when the principle of honouring the Sacred Feminine is abandoned. Thus the spider's parlour is created, and awaits its predator and its victim.

The desecration, rape and pillage of the planet itself is connected to the attitude that is informed, encouraged and fomented by the forces that comprise pornography. And the indifference and cruelty to animals that we see across the world is the result of the pathological inability to feel, which is promoted by the menacing ethics behind the mass consumption of pornography.

It is time to investigate the case of the Faceless Woman.

The Faceless Woman

Discussing the above issues with a male friend, he, on reflection, agreed that there certainly were psychological elements of rapaciousness and the savouring of the reduction of women to sexual enslavement in the use of pornography. He became determined to eliminate pornographic attitudes from his sexuality.

Since the beginning of his use of pornography as a boy,

a woman had visited him in his dreams and brought him to orgasm. She was tall and very slender, naked, with long black hair. He never saw her face, but was involved only with the use of her body. More than two decades after her first appearance, she was still visiting him several times a week. He decided to begin his move towards emancipation by dealing with her.

I suggested, trying to be helpful, that he should look her in the eyes and ask her name when she next appeared. He duly attempted this, but could see no eyes and in fact no face at all. We consulted his spirit guide, who has proved on numerous occasions to be unfailingly trustworthy and accurate in the advice he offers. My friend's spirit guide explained that the woman had no face and no name. She was not real in the way that other astral entities are. She had been created as an amalgam of every time my friend had looked at a woman with a dehumanizing, pornographic intent, particularly when this chosen route to erotic feelings culminated in masturbation.

She was drawing her motive force from the dark whirl-pool of pornographic energy previously mentioned, via his contribution to it.

My friend began his campaign by refusing the faceless woman's advances. She became aggressive and very deter-mined. My friend grew more and more aware of her strange unrealness, although in an experiential sense she was very real indeed.

He noted, for instance, how her body, though 'perfect', was exactly like the artificial, air-brushed appearance of women's bodies in explicit magazines.

Finally, after a titanic struggle, the faceless woman was permanently driven from his dreams. She thereafter made an appearance in my friend's waking psychic vision, constantly pursuing him. She seemed to lead him into every situation possible where an opportunity of degrading his sexuality might occur, from inadvertently parking in 'dogger' territory, to drawing up next to a skip full of discarded pornography, and being assailed by young prostitutes exposing their breasts and begging for business! By denying the faceless woman, he had reaped the full fury of the whirlwind or, more accurately, the dark whirlpool. Every time that these events occurred, the faceless woman waited in the wings, desperate for him to re-enter her domain. However, there was no human feeling within the scope of her consciousness, but just a need for power and domination.

On one occasion, when she had beckoned to him to look in the aforementioned skip and, listening to his account of these strange events over the telephone, I had urged him to do so, melodramatically imagining he might find a dead body, she seemed angry when he returned to his vehicle empty-handed after discovering a bundle of pornography. Soon afterwards a man appeared who dumped some rubbish into the skip.

When he spotted the pornography, he retrieved a pile of magazines and walked back to his car, apparently without noticing that he had dropped a few of them along the way. As he drove off, my friend saw a faceless woman running after him, distinct from his own by her long red hair and slightly different body shape, but similar in all other respects.

The dropped magazines were directly in front of my friend's vehicle. A wind got up from nowhere and turned their pages. He looked on, refusing to connect with them.

After this, the faceless woman disappeared and pursued him no more.

My friend has continued to see the phenomenon of the faceless woman, although not his own, but those of other people. Disturbingly, the faceless women gather round and pursue young boys as well as older youths and men. Even at a relatively tender age they have been accumulating. My friend has also perceived them in pursuit of girls and women. Their attraction of the faceless women seemed not to arise from a lesbian interest, but from a blatant support and encouragement of the sexual degradation and slavery inherent in pornography.

The purpose bound into the entity of the faceless woman, which has its source in the deepest-rooted darkness that is, very literally, the direst enemy of humankind (there is also a profoundly beautiful darkness), is to prevent the Sacred Marriage from occurring between men and women, and between lesbian and gay partners, who are exploring aspects of the Sacred Marriage from a different but equally important perspective, and who contribute to it in every way as much as heterosexual partners when the relationships of both are in balance and harmoniously attuned to the principles of the Sacred Marriage.

Without the Sacred Marriage, everything eventually goes wrong, the centre cannot hold, and creation cannot sustain itself beyond a certain point. But it is a prerequisite that the Sacred Marriage must take place between the Sacred Feminine and Sacred Masculine principles when they are in perfect harmony. One cannot be degraded, veiled and enslaved, and the other abusive and dominant. Such a union produces death, not life. It is not possible to sow tares and gather corn.

The two divine centres that the faceless woman encourages her creators to spiritually desecrate and deny are the heart centre and the sacral centre, dwelling at the position of the breasts and the vulva. One enshrines the mystery of the heart, and the other the mystery of spiritual vision and divinely enlightened percipience known as the Khem or Chem (see Chapter Eight). These reveal the wonder of the Sacred Feminine, and it is only by deep attunement to her mysteries and the resultant profound understanding of them that men can discover and centre themselves in their own inheritance of the Sacred Masculine. This is why the faceless woman stands like the fabled 'Dweller on the Threshold', blinding, barring and blocking the way to these two routes to percipience. When they are so hidden, barred and blocked, the intelligent awareness that is the head centre – the receiving and coordinating station for the sacral and heart centres – remains vacant and disconnected, as though without eyes or a face. And, of course, the fact that the woman manifests without eyes or a face is a blatant result of the dehumanizing of women created by pornographic attitudes.

There is no doubt that the faceless woman is a malignant entity. We must understand that she is a human creation, and also that we have the ability to create, for we are made in the image of the Creator. Her brief is to lead her charges into ever deeper and more sinister pornographic territory (although soft porn is in itself very dangerous and harmful territory). The general effect is like a drug, where the fix becomes less and less effective. As this happens, the faceless woman begins to change, like an imago emerging from its chrysalis. Her new form is too repugnant and eerie to linger over, but it is certainly very horrifying and emits an icy, rapacious, ravaging evil.

Even as I write this, a man is appearing on television insisting that if women cover up, then the issue of pornographic consumption of their image and the issues surrounding it, such as sexual violence, would significantly decrease. Apart from the numerous feminist concerns that such a stance invokes, the healing balance of the Sacred Marriage can never be found while women are insistently regarded as expressions of either the Whore or the Virgin. The laws of justice and human rights are not served by insisting that, unless a woman stays locked in her tower, the wolves will devour her. Holding women at bay because of their sexuality is the root of the problem.

Nevertheless, the problem has to be tackled, not only by men, but by women, too. As women, we need to learn again how to express our sexuality in all its power, dignity and beauty (whether or not flesh is 'exposed' is an irrelevance) and as a force of our potent spirituality, rather than making it an expression of slavery, indignity, and collusion with the male drive to dehumanize and dominate.

The point is not that eroticism itself should be lessened in intensity or force. Our capacity for erotic expression is part of our spirituality and a means by which we embrace and understand hidden things. When it is a component of a harmonious whole it is a revelation of the mysteries of love and forms a vehicle for their highest expression. In the Gospel of Philip, discovered among the Gnostic gospels, one of the teachings of Christ is that the power of properly attuned coitus is vast. The problem arises when eroticism becomes separated from the heart and becomes predatory and self-gratifying. When eroticism is separated from the heart, from the powers of love and wisdom that endow it with its true motive force, its considerable conductive potency for life and the expansion of love goes into reversal. The result is extremely dangerous and destructive. A myriad Belle de Jours signalling to the collective mentality that such a separated force of eroticism is fun, glamorous, diverting and harmless cannot change what it becomes. Such persuasion is a puppet-master lie.

The discoverer of the faceless woman overcame the forces that animated her by one simple resolve – to allow his sensitivity to the beauty of women to be received in his heart rather than bypassing this centre and going straight to his genitals. In this way, he stopped 'beheading' himself in his perception of the Sacred Feminine and became a true Templar or Gentle Man: one who honours and does not betray and abuse the power and mystery of the Sacred Feminine.

Beheading was an important symbol among the Templars, for they knew that within the heart lies a centre of consciousness that William Blake called the organ of 'pure reason'. It is the point of supreme intelligence within, as if it were the spiritual brain.

Unless the head centre works with this point of supreme intelligence, nothing can be properly understood. That is why our scientists and medical researchers can never quite grasp the greater answers that they seek, for they reject the truth which would so readily conjoin its hand with theirs. When the consciousness in the head bypasses the heart and links with other centres of awareness, the resulting intelligence is not 'pure reason' but 'guileful wisdom', the treachery to which Mary Magdalene alerted us and which leads us straight into the jaws of Enlil's dark plan. When the head centre is cut off from the heart centre, we are beheaded. The result of a failed Sacred Marriage is a beheading.

The experience of eroticism is magnified and intensified to a supreme ecstasy when we use it with correct attunement – an erotic ecstasy unconscionably more potent than anything that pornography could engender. It is from this ecstasy that the true power of coitus arises, a power that goes beyond even the miracle of physical conception. It is a treasure-house of wondrous provisions waiting to be unlocked and unloaded. Its stores will change the world.

To experience life and to occupy the dimensions which the Ka angels, in their desire for our liberation and our greatest good, wish us to experience and occupy, we need to conceive of an approach to sexuality and eroticism that is very different to the distorted, enslaved, vulgarized and squalid projections of these forces that surround us today. Simple rites to Anahita can help us to achieve this.

Anahita

Anahita would call us back in memory to a time when women were given power, perhaps not over men, but rather *in* men. We might say that this was at the very beginning of creation of the human concept in God's heart.

Woman was the holder of a certain divine essence that originates in the female because it originated in the source of Mother God, the Source of All. It has to be given to men by women, as Mother God gave it to Father God, because he was of her very essence. It is known throughout folklore as 'the living waters', and it manifests in the 'Dew-Cup' known to the alchemists. Menstruation is a physical symbol expressive of this most holy principle. It is called 'Star Fire', because it is the spiritual essence of the stars and the starry wisdom within the ancient starlight. The stars are fiery beings of the sacred dragon, born from the Mother's heart. We are all children of the stars. Every element that composes us was created in the divine alchemical laboratory of the constellations. Stellar light nourishes us, stellar embodiment creates us. The tides of life itself flow to us from the stars.

Derdekea

There is a great being that encompasses the spectrum of angelic, human and divine potencies. She is known as Derdekea, the Drop, for she is a drop of God's pure, distilled essence. She is a manifestation of the sacred living waters and the ineffable fire that coruscates through them whose play gives birth to creation. She is the signature of all fruitfulness and fertility, encompassing the profoundest heights and depths of what these qualities convey. It is she who is Mistress of the Grail. She is, in her deepest essence, the Grail itself. She is the Divine Daughter who will lead us back to a proper realization of the Mother, not as someone in brackets standing by as a subordinate to a masculine God who is the Creator, waiting to facilitate 'His' creation by embodying it, but as the Source and the All. She is the hidden or veiled aspect of Brigid, what we do not yet understand and realize about the greatness of Brigid. It is she whom Anahita serves. Look into the eyes of Anahita and you will find the mystery of Derdekea dwelling therein.

Rite to Anahita

To enter into the simple rites to Anahita, repeat the preparatory steps as usual:

Find a quiet place, or withdraw deep into the privacy and quietude within yourself.

Ask for the protection of Archangels Michael and Shekinah.

Make a request to your guardian angel to be linked safely, securely and harmoniously with Anahita.

Let your focus gently touch your heart, and allow your mind to rest there.

In an act of imagination, let your breath rise and fall through your heart.

Breathe slowly and easily, letting the rhythm of your breath bring you peace.

Let that point of peace fill you with light as if it were a shining star.

Know that your breath is magical, and will take you deeper into the light.

Begin to see Anahita, 'the immaculate one, genius of fertilizing water and of the fruitfulness of the earth'. She appears as if out of shining morning mists, as if she is arising from the sea or from still, clear inland waters. Pure white vapours separate to reveal her radiant, smiling form.

Say her name softly three times, in love and greeting.

Become aware of a rainbow bridge at your feet. It glimmers softly with the seven rays of creation. It leads into Anahita's heart. Step onto the bridge. Walk forward and enter into the mid-point of Anahita's perfect light.

Feel a welcome, a sense of encompassing love, and a buoyant joy that lifts you further into the glory of her light as she encloses you in her being. Feel the delight of dwelling in the sacred centre. Rest in the incomparable light.

Anahita is becoming a tree of pure light. The light is clear, like a brilliant glassy wave. The light is golden, like the midday sun shining at the zenith of a perfect Edenic day. The light is pure, bright white, like a sacred unicorn bearing the light of God.

You, within her, are becoming a tree formed from that unutterable light. You become a tree of light with Anahita.

A tracery of light forms your crown. Boughs of light stretch out in loving embrace of the universal spirit. Your trunk is strong and gracious. Your roots penetrate far into the secret depths of the earth, where there are countless wonders. A great being of light dwells within the earth, cloaked from our outer perception but not from the wisdom of the heart. She enshrines the mystery of the Sacred Feminine, glorious, bright 'beyond the cities of the imperishable stars'. It is within her divine mystery that Anahita has her roots, and you have your roots. Let the wondrous light move through you. Be a tree of light.

Above you and beneath you dwells the mystery of the Sacred Feminine. Let that mystery travel up and down the steadfast column of your mighty trunk. It is a serpent of light, descending and rising like a living fountain. Let it come to rest in the sanctity of your heart. And at that holy point of fusion, let it become a rose.

The rose is hallowed and emits a purity of fragrance, the perfume of pristine creation. It is like tender words spoken in the depths of your being. A veil is drawn aside, and you see that the rose enshrines a jewel in its immaculate heart.

Take the jewel. It is yours to become consummate with. It shines in your hand. It is a golden apple. Lift it to your lips. Bite into it.

The sweetness that fills you changes your perception and lifts you into exalted vision. The bitten apple has become a cup, wondrous, beauteous: a dragon cup, carved from the essence of every precious thing throughout creation. It mirrors a mystery, a secret that lies within your own being, as though inside you dwelt the universe, and this was its ineffable source, the holy of holies.

Within the cup is a drop of dew. It is from the rose. It was placed in the cup by the apple. Its essence enshrines your Pendragon self. It is yours to drink.

Lift the cup; drink; take from the dragon cup and drink down its dew.

The words of a prayer like silver-winged angels take form in the sacred cavern of your mouth. Speak the prayer:

Anahita, radiant and blessed,
lovely and deep-moving among the joys of
   the angels,
cleanse my soul from its roots to its crown
with the bright light of the Sacred Tree.
Bring purity to my heart
with the fragrance of the mystical rose.
Make my perception inviolate
with the drop of holy dew from Derdekea's
   dragon cup.
Let me become in every degree
My Pendragon self
Lit with the noble flame of God's presence.

Thank Anahita for the gifts she bestows on you, and for her loving service.

Softly reconnect with the earth by sitting quietly for a moment or two and envisioning strong roots, like tree roots, growing down from the soles of your feet into the ground until they reach the heart of the earth. Let them anchor firmly there.

See a vivid white-silver cross in a ring of light touch and glow out from the crown of your head, the top of your forehead at its centre point, the brow ridge above your nose, the hollow of your throat, your heart, your solar plexus, just below your navel and at the bottom of your spine at the point of the tail bone.

Ask Anahita to be with you as you move through your day. Receive her blessings – and her challenges – like a true Pendragon.

Chapter Twenty

HAURVATAT, ANGEL OF WHOLENESS

The name of this great angel may seem a little strange. It is good to know that the angels are not fastidious on points of pronunciation! What is important is simply to dwell easily on any angelic name that seems difficult, and allow its structure to form a rhythm in your mind that flows and is pleasing to you. My rendition of Haurvatat, for instance, is 'hour' with a sounded 'h', followed by 'var-tat'. This may not be right for you, but with a little experimentation you will discover what is.

Haurvatat manifests to the inner vision as a mighty feminine angel. She is the personification of salvation. Zoroastrianism designates her 'the spirit of the waters', and it is interesting to think of her in connection with the mysteries of the Arthurian Lady of the Lake, who inspired and guided King Arthur and Camelot. Scholarship, particularly that of Philip Gardiner and Gary Osborn, has verified a strong association with Brigid and this mysterious Lady of the waters.

Anahita shares these same associations with Haurvatat. Like Anahita, Haurvatat works with and serves Derdekea. These four feminine great ones, Brigid, Derdekea, Anahita and Haurvatat, combine their essence to create a mighty temple of the Sacred Feminine, of Goddess, that overlights the earth. And so Haurvatat's presence is overarching, like the grandeur, peace and sanctity of a cathedral.

If we did not have cathedrals upon the earth, we would not so readily understand the divine calm and majesty of heaven that pours through Haurvatat, Keeper of the Temple of the Sacred Feminine. If, when you think of her, you think of the sanctified interior of a cathedral, free from the earthly strife and constriction surrounding systems of faith, you will easily sense the overarching presence of Haurvatat.

Haurvatat has dominion over the wholeness and goodness of life and its expression. She is mistress of flourishing vegetation and radiant health. Mani, who initiated the Mandean cult as a new interpretation of Zoroastrianism, translated Haurvatat into her masculine aspect of Harudha, who afterwards became familiar as the European Green Man. Perhaps this is why the Green Man image appears unfailingly among cathedral decorative carvings – as a mirror of Haurvatat, star of the Sacred Feminine and spirit of the waters.

Although Haurvatat encompasses many dimensions and our communion with her is not in any way limited, her Ka angel aspect at this time seems to be involved very much with our use of language. Our use of language goes hand in hand with our emotional and mental perception and the nature and generation of our thoughts. These three great Titans of the structure of our being cannot be separated. They all interplay and feed one another. They are the tributaries that create the active body of our deeds and actions, our expression of life.

The words that we choose to speak carry great power. We can use these vast reserves of potency to serve the light or to serve the darkness, and in fact are constantly doing so, whether or not we bother to monitor or influence the process of their bias.

Haurvatat says:

> The time during which human souls believed that it was sufficient to want good on earth and good for their fellows only in a general and philosophical sense without looking to their own individual output of light or darkness must now end.
>
> The time has come for each soul to examine and monitor and filter in detail the quality and direction of their every step along the four great paths of service that encompass the spheres of perception, thought, word and deed. They correlate to the four elements of your being. Perception, or vision, equates to fire and is your passage to the fifth element, the quintessence. Thought equates to air; word correlates to the music and flow of water; deed equates to earth. They are how your world is created and sustained in its creation.
>
> Without attention to these four vital paths, the good-intentioned will find themselves swept away on a tide manipulated by the powers of darkness. Call on us in your endeavours. We are here to help you. We will lift you into triumph.

We were each born wielding the power of the mage. Our magicianhood is our birthright. Our magical command lies in our thoughts and our words. It is an unlimited power, a power so great that when we begin to exercise it in the light of our Pendragon self, we will be astounded, almost embarrassed, by the scope and wonder of the generative and creative power that we hold.

There is much dross and degeneration in our use of language at the present point in human history. Much of it is random, thoughtless and abusive. Having been freed from the strictures of Victorian censorship which nurtured the shock element in language (a most unwise power to hand to the manipulative forces.), we have chosen a western culture which refers constantly to the Sacred Marriage and the Mother principle in abusive and obscene terms. The idea that this is 'powerful' language is constantly reinforced. We are warned, for instance, that the use of 'strong' language is involved in what we are about to view or read, as if the absence of such continual strikes and attacks is a rendition of 'weak' language!

There is, of course, much, much more to the use of powerful language than refraining from obscenities. However, the framework of our use of language has been so invaded by their automatic and consequently robotic use that it is necessary to clear a way through the debris to a point where we can become powerful again. The following exercise has been found to be helpful in casting off the hypnotic, addictive and persuasive qualities in what actually oppresses and poisons. It is known as 'the Dance of the Two Dragons' or 'Archangel Michael's Purifying Fire'. (This exercise is also given in my book, *Angel Healing*).

The ceremony takes the form of an initiation, and although it sounds alarming, it is perfectly safe. It involves calling forth the holy fire of Michael, from just below the feet to the area above the crown, until we are cleansed of all accumulated dross and contaminated psychic matter.

Simultaneously, we call upon our own Pendragon essence to come forth. This purifying fire of Michael that summons the Pendragon or heart-flame essence to flood our being is the Light of Brigid. Although the fire of Michael performs the task, it is Brigid's radiance that is finally evoked.

The Dance of the Two Dragons

Create the star in the heart with your imagination. Let it grow until it contains you in its heart. Stand within the protection of the star throughout this ceremony.

Say: 'Archangel Michael, Angelic Lord of Fire, be with me and protect me during this ritual. Brigid, Mistress of the Pure Flame, please bless and oversee my endeavour. I open my heart to your essence and welcome you in'

Hold forth your right hand, and see an unlit torch there in your grasp.

Say: 'Archangel Michael, light my torch with heavenly fire!'

See the torch blazing with spiritual fire. Its glory outshines the sun.

Say: 'This ignited torch is my higher will. With it I invoke the spiritual fire to take light at my feet, and engulf each of my subtle bodies in purifying, renewing flame.'

Lower the torch to your feet, letting it rest there. See a glowing spiritual fire spring to life beneath your feet. See its tongues of flame rise in a great column around you.

Stand in its brilliant centre, letting them sweep through you, hearing the roaring song of the flames as they take into themselves all the contaminated energy that has burdened you for so long. Rejoice in this cleansing, knowing that your heart embraces it, and it is what your spirit longs for.

As the flames dance around you, know that you are truly a dragon, a creature of spiritual fire. Like King Arthur, you are the Pendragon, the Head Dragon. Feel the flames revolving around your head, like a coronet of most holy light. That is your higher dragon essence, rising from your heart and dancing in a ring of ecstasy through and around your higher chakras.

Now see a writhing dragon in the flames under your feet,

where you placed your torch. This is your lower dragon, the dragon of your dark, limited, unlit self; and it will writhe in pain until you deliver it from suffering by striking it through with your golden lance, your heavenly self that is contained in the dancing dragon of the supernal heights that gyrates around you.

Reach into your deepest heart, your highest dragon essence, and bring forth the golden lance, the ramrod of light that glances and flashes with divine fire, the inconceivable fire of Goddess-God that only your most exalted vision can delineate.

Plunge this lance into the dragon at your feet.

The lower dragon ceases its anguished writhing, and, charged with the dynamic energy of the higher dragon, begins to spiral upward in coils of light. It meets the Pendragon, and both enter a balletic sequence of supreme joy. The higher and the lower dragon merge in the Pendragon's pure golden light.

This is your heart-light. It is pulsating love, the love which creates, informs and sustains the universe.

You and your higher dragon are one; and the higher dragon has absorbed the lower dragon.

After a minute or so, let the dragons disappear into the furnace, and the furnace disappear into the light of the star. Let the star recede until it becomes again the radiant jewel in your heart centre.

Thank Brigid and Archangel Michael for their protection and blessing, and end the ceremony by sealing your chakras with the symbol of a bright silver cross in a ring of light (each arm of the cross touches the circumference of the circle). (See the end of the previous chapter if you are unsure of the location of the chakras.)

The mysterious connection between water and words is demonstrated in the fascinating story of the Japanese scientist, Masaru Emoto. Again, the 'mother tongue' reveals its secret course through the living heart of language, for emotion (Emoto) is connected with the element of water, and in their finer essence the two are one.

Dr Emoto's exciting studies began when he met Dr Lee H. Lorenzen, a biochemist at the University of California who later became a water researcher and went on to develop Magnetic Resonance Water. He was able to provide Dr Emoto with a special piece of equipment called a Magnetic Resonance Analyzer, which could actually measure and demonstrate subtle energy via the medium of water. Dr Emoto began his experiments in this field and published numerous academic works on his findings relating to 'Hado', which is the Japanese term for the world of subtle energy relating to consciousness.

Meanwhile, Dr Emoto had learned that, although there has been snowfall on planet Earth for many millions of years, no two snow crystals comprising the flakes are ever the same shape, just as no two human beings are ever exactly alike, except in the specified case of identical twins. In other words, snow crystals, synonymous with the molecular structure of water, are like humans in that they possess individuality. Their faces are never the same!

Dr Emoto wanted to find a way not only of measuring and demonstrating the intelligent flow of subtle energy in water with a physical instrument, as he had been doing, but of actually capturing its 'faces' to see what the water was imparting and conveying through its subtle energy intelligence or consciousness.

He hit upon the idea of freezing the water under

experimentation, and then taking pictures of the crystals made by the frozen water. The results were both astounding and stunning.

The first thing of wonder he discovered was that, at the precise moment directly before frozen water melts and returns to its fluid form, it invariably creates a shape identical to the Chinese character denoting 'water'. It must have felt to Dr Emoto as if the water was introducing itself, saying, 'Hello. I am Water...' And, of course, it is yet another demonstration of the versatility and sheer unexpectedness of the presence of the 'mother tongue'.

Further experiments proved that water produced the most exquisite crystalline structures as a form of natural expression, except in cases where it was polluted or disinfected, in which case the breathtaking images, originally like ethereal crop circles or jewels created by angelic crystal-smiths, broke down into distressing and ugly patterns painful to behold.

The real breakthrough, from the stance of the teaching of the Ka angels regarding our human use of language, came when Dr Emoto chanced on the idea of writing words on waxed paper and leaving them in water overnight. On freezing and photographing the resultant crystalline structures or 'faces' of the water, he was able to measure the actual effect of the words chosen.

Where a positive word conveying a beautiful energy or concept was placed in the water, such as 'joy' or 'peace' or 'love', or even 'beauty' itself, the water exploded into crystalline patterns of wonder.

Starry configurations of exquisite flower forms and jewel facets composed themselves into structures of surpassing harmony and mystical architecture, as if, using Dr Emoto's expression, they were a 'prayer to beauty'.

However, when words of negativity or abuse were left to infuse the water with their emanations, the crystalline structures showed patterns of misery, disintegration and squalor, of distortion and dissonance: lurid murky mutations like rotting and crumbling masonry or earthquake rubble, or just a dying away into stagnation and corruption and terrible disfigurement.

So there we have it. Undeniable, incontrovertible, cast-iron proof that the way we use language, the words we speak, actually impact ourselves and our environment in a dramatic and definite way. Not only do these emanations impact our environment and reality, they actually *create* and *reconfigure* it. Because of the ubiquitous nature of subtle energy, we permeate and suffuse everything that surrounds us, even the very air we breathe, with the impress of the energy we release through our language. And that energy is intelligent. It creates and invigorates, or it pollutes and destroys, according to our choice.

Of course, Dr Emoto's work is wider ranging even than this devastating revelation, because it also proves the traumatic effects of pollution and environmental destruction on our world – the power of perception, thought and deed as well as the power of the word. His books are a treasure-house of innovation and inspiration.

Nevertheless, the insight he provides into the awesome power of the words we use every day is a shocking and a sobering one.

If we could really take on board in the entirety of its meaning the full implication of what his work has revealed, surely we would in all circumstances rather be silent and clamp down on our tongue a thousand times a day than to speak words of hatred, spite, criticism, despair, ill omen and abuse as we do habitually, carelessly, obliviously, unthinkingly and unheedingly. For what we put out comes back to us like a homing bird. We breathe, eat and drink the energy we have chosen, for good or for ill. It is one of the most alarming aspects of karma that we can contemplate.

Of course, the angels, especially the Ka angels, understand that we are human. Sometimes it is necessary to unburden the soul, because denial of pain, sorrow or anger is never the answer. However, it is essential to bear in mind that, in thus unburdening ourselves, we are unloading in order to take on calmer, purer, happier energies. If there is no helpful human companion available, we can always call on the angels. Also, it is astonishing how animals naturally show sympathy, followed by positivity, when we verbally and emotionally unburden to them. We are not called on to be terrified prisoners of language! It is just a case of monitoring and filtering, followed by purposeful guidance and direction, as Haurvatat explains.

Nonetheless, we have to put our heads and hearts into gear to achieve this. We have to seek alert awareness, we have to strive to remember. There are forces which will do all in their considerable power to push us into forgetfulness and lethargy.

Haurvatat will help us on all fronts. She creates the heavenly vault in which the sacred word is sounded. She will endow us with a guard to set over our tongue.

To enter into her rites, prepare as always:

The Rite of Haurvatat

Find a quiet place, or withdraw deep into the privacy and quietude within yourself.

Ask for the protection of Archangels Michael and Shekinah.

Make a request to your guardian angel to be linked safely, securely and harmoniously with Anahita.

Let your focus gently touch your heart, and allow your mind to rest there.

In an act of imagination, let your breath rise and fall through your heart.

Breathe slowly and easily, letting the rhythm of your breath bring you peace.

Let that point of peace fill you with light as if it were a shining star.

Know that your breath is magical, and will take you deeper into the light.

Call on Haurvatat. Sound her name three times.

Begin to see Haurvatat with mighty white wings, enfolding you in her grace. She holds you in the sanctity of her light. Her beautiful, kindly countenance expresses a peace that is vast and hushed and timeless, because it descends from the heart of God, from Divine Mother.

Make your request to her, using these words or your own:

> Haurvatat, Blessed One from the shining
>   realms,
> set a guard over my tongue for all time, so that
>   no
> unthinking words should fall from my lips.
> Inspire my words always with your fruitfulness
>   of
> wholesome grace and the guidance of your
>   kindly light.

See Haurvatat raise her hands over you in blessing, and then draw them together as if in prayer. She opens her hands and places a white rose of unearthly beauty in the hollow of your throat. Let your heart connect with it and send its perfect fragrance to your brow and crown centres. Sense its perfume rising like temple incense. See the white rose dwelling in the hollow of your throat like a healing touch.

Haurvatat communicates to you in the cathedral hush of her magical presence that the white rose will always be there, blessing and purifying the energy flow of your language. You need only connect with it and know that it is there from time to time to keep it in its dwelling place. She bids you see it in your mind's eye. She says to you:

> Whenever the purity of your language energy stream is threatened, while the words are still silent and taking form, a golden sword will arise from the golden stamens at the white rose's heart. It will arise as if from a lake, like Excalibur. Take that sword and hold it against the out-spill that threatens as if you held a divine symbol against the darkness.
>
> The invading words and negative intent will disappear into the rose and be absorbed by it into the unassailable purity of its essence.

The golden sword is generated by Haurvatat, and the light issuing from it strikes the inner eye with a brightness as white as lilies. Yet its wielding and protection is of Michael. It is made of Haurvatat's light, but its forging into a sword is done by Michael. It is Archangel Michael's sword, but if you look into its heart, you see that it is formed from Haurvatat's light, which is the Light of Brigid. This is the mystery of Archangel Michael's sword, as it was and is the mystery of Excalibur.

Now Haurvatat lifts you deeper into her light. Feel it cascading down on you and running through you in waves of pure delight, like rills of water. Realize that you are chakra-bathing. Each chakra is being washed and energized by Haurvatat's beautiful light of heaven. It is a rapturous, invigorating experience. Feel the play and plash of the ethereal water as it rushes over and under your feet and then rises like a serpent of clear spiralling light to wash through your base chakra at the bottom of the spine, your sacral chakra beneath your navel, your solar plexus chakra, your heart chakra, your throat chakra, then across your eyes in a cool and soothing surge like a soft caress, upward around your brow chakra in laughing swirls, rising to your unicorn's horn chakra at the top of the forehead in the middle, your crown chakra, the chakra at the base of your brain, and then down your arms to your hands, around which it plays in beautiful ripples as it does about your feet. Enjoy the magical revivification of this gentle, life-giving torrent.

Haurvatat lifts a cup to your lips. It is the dragon cup, containing the mystical drop. Look into the cup. You will see that it contains the Word, from which everything sprang, creation in its pristine morning loveliness. Gaze into the depths of the cup.

Become one with the Word, for the Word is you. Its power dwells within you. It is the gift of God, for you to use as you will.

Drink from the cup. Take its essence into you. Know that the cup and its essence are one ineffable whole, and when you drink the essence, you become the cup.

Haurvatat places the Dragon Cup into your heart. There it will always reside as your gift of consciousness of the Word and its sublime power.

Thank Haurvatat for her ministrations. Let her cloak you with her graciousness, so that you carry it back with you to normal consciousness.

Affirm your Pendragon self, so that you are centred in it. 'I am the Pendragon, and I stand in the light of my Pendragon self.'

See a vivid white-silver cross in a ring of light touch and glow out from the crown of your head, the top of your forehead at its centre point, the brow ridge above your nose, the hollow of your throat, your heart, your solar plexus, just below your navel and at the bottom of your spine at the point of the tail bone.

Affirm your Pendragonhood once again, and go forth into your day, carrying Haurvatat's blessing with you.

Chapter Twenty-One

THE HUMAN DRAGON

We have journeyed far with the Ka angels. We have entered deep into their domain and invited them into ours. It is time now, should you feel that it is right for you, to transform into your Pendragon self.

It is not too melodramatic to say that we are engaged on a mission. Our mission involves coming to the aid of humanity and the planet. Each of us must play our part. The Ka angels urge us on, but gently, angelically, keeping the balance. They know that those who are attuned to the light must carry this mission through, and that there is an exact mathematical calculation involved before what some term 'critical mass' can occur. Opinions vary, but one figure put forward is that the ratio required to reach 'critical mass' is one light worker per 10,000 people. This proportion of workers centred in the light and projecting it into the darkest places, ensuring that the light is accessible to those who are struggling, will make it possible for the forces of light to begin to dismantle the dark global empire of war and greed that persists at the moment. Indeed, although we have not quite reached the point of 'critical mass' just yet, the collapse of this sinister empire has already begun.

Having worked and celebrated with the Ka angels, having sought to manifest gold in the crucible throughout rites designed to prepare the human soul in thought, word and perception, it is time now to attune to the magic of the spirit with regard to our deeds and actions in the outer world.

We have seen how Enlil, the ill-willed brother of the two who came to the planet in the early days of our world, gained unlawful ascendancy over his light-attuned brother, Enki, who wished nothing but good for humankind; and how it is vital to overturn the dark plans that Enlil has laid for us. The wives of both brothers are crucial to the story in every sense, but have been obscured and veiled.

One of the great foci among our tasks must be to restore the Sacred Feminine to the earth in all her potency and glory. Women, for many ages, have not been all that Goddess intended for them. She made us in her own image, and we must reclaim that birthright before the earth can be healed. We are waiting to be born, to struggle out into the light of day and truly attain our womanhood. When we have rescued this honour, when the unicorn is crowned once more (for the heraldic image of the lion and the unicorn, sacred masculine and sacred feminine, shows the lion as crowned, while the crown of the unicorn has slipped from its rightful position down to the base of her horn), when women step into their own and make good their heritage, transformation can begin.

We need to remember these things as we seek to become the Pendragon. Formerly, this being of light has been associated only with a masculine identity. But it is important to be aware, on entering into Pendragonhood, that our Mother God was known originally as the great Dragon Queen, the Source, the Originator, and the All.

The second thing we must remember as we set out on the mission of restoring our own Dragonhood is that Enlil has no power over us. This may seem a strange assertion when we look out on the world and see him riding so high on the cusp of the waves of power. Everywhere, it seems, Enlil has made his mark and claimed his dominion.

Yet it is true to say that he may wield over us only that measure of power which we, consciously or unconsciously, are willing to give into his hands.

Enlil has created a terrible smoke-demon of fear which oppresses and demoralizes us. As the human spearhead of all the confusion, anxiety and darkness of the material world, he can only too easily seem all-powerful. It is what he strives to make us think.

But in actual fact, he is impotent. The death-forces he embraces are, to state a truism, without life. They have no impetus of creativity. Of course, this does not mean to say that if we make a gift to him of *our* life and creativity, he cannot capitalize on them to the highest degree. He still has some control over our karma, for he was once, in his early days as a reasonably benign leader, a lesser lord of karma, although the judgment aspect of a lord of karma has been removed from him entirely. What he can do, and revels in so doing, is to hurl at us devastating thunderbolts of the negative karma we ourselves create. He cannot operate outside cosmic law, but he can apply it in such a way as to make life much darker and more distressing and difficult for us here on earth than it was ever intended to be.[4]

The initial step on our journey, therefore, is to cut Enlil down to size and to reclaim the 'I Am' that exists within us. We do this very simply, through the breath. We may think of the House of Shimtî, meaning 'breath-wind-life',

---

4 The full story of Enki and Enlil, and how they have shaped our world, is told in *The Secret of the Ages –The Discovery of the Holy Grail*.

Nin-Khursag and Enki's miraculous 'creation chamber' in which the first earthly human beings came to life, designated as such because it contained the essence of, and linked them to, God.

The breath is deeply magical and, if we would become dragons, we need to know how to use it. We need to breathe fire – the right sort of fire, which is light. As dragons, we breathe easily and without effort from the centre of our bodies, yet ensuring that we gently fill our lungs to their capacity, and peacefully empty them (we cannot entirely empty them, because a small residue of air must always remain within the lungs). In doing this, people sometimes find it easier to visualize their lungs filling with air and expanding to the sides, rather than thrusting out at the front of the body. We focus on our breath to calm and steady the mind.

We now attune to the 'I Am', the great 'Aum' of Buddhism. When we assert our 'I-Am' selves, we begin to stimulate the divine inner fires, which allow us to assume our true Dragonhood. Enlil, we must remember, wants to force us into our lower saurian-hood, whereby we become the tortured dragon of wrath bound on the wheel of its own self-destruction, the opposite of the divine Ouroboros, the dragon forming the ring of light, which is associated with Enki. This wrath-dragon of the lower self is an entirely earthbound creature, sub-human and divested of all the magnificence of its spiritual heritage. We tame it with the breath and the reclaiming of the 'I Am', which allows the royal dragon, the Pendragon, to come into its own.

We now choose any quality of the higher self of which we stand in particular need. It might be courage or strength, peace or harmony, love or kindness, patience or endurance, clarity or joy – any one of a vast number of exalted spiritual states which we are finding difficult to achieve or maintain. We then intone the simple mantra:

I AM Divine Peace

or:

I AM Divine Love

or:

I AM Divine Wisdom

or whatever it is that you feel you need in order to banish the shadows from your life. The mantra is said while focusing on your breathing and on your words. Say it peacefully, slowly, powerfully. Say it many times, until it becomes a rhythm pulsing through your mind, effortless, resonant, musical.

There is a special form of the 'I Am' that is particularly potent. It is the mantra of the Holy Grail because, of course, the Grail is the Resurrection, our own personal resurrection from the tomb in which Enlil has sought to constrict us for so long: the rolling away of the Stone of Death from the door of our prison:

I AM the Resurrection and the Life.

Naturally, the 'I AM' is not a reference to the little self of earth, to which feelings of grandiose self-importance might attach themselves. The 'I AM' is our God-self, our Pendragon self, which cannot be swayed by petty egotism, but remains always noble, always humble. Because it is centred in humility, humiliation cannot wound it. Select a mantra and repeat it for a few minutes each day, or whenever you have need of it. Thus will you begin to re-establish the power of the dragon that Enlil has sought to leach away from you, and that the angels are determined to return to you.

In dealing with the ego, we also need to remember that the tools Enlil has employed most diligently to confuse us consist of blame, self-righteousness and revenge or punishment.

We must above all things refuse their employment. When astonishing and staggering revelations come to light, as they will, about our governments and authoritarian bodies, we must not turn on them in blame and hatred. This would be to give Enlil his eleventh-hour coup d'état. Instead, it is vital to focus only on love, forgiveness, reconciliation, inclusion, upliftment into the light. In this way, all humanity will be called home.

To become dragons, we also need to reclaim the unwavering gaze of the dragon, by means of which it can control its own inner cosmos, and work spiritual miracles within its own environment. This unwavering gaze is the focus of the mind; and it is the mind we must learn to still and strengthen, so that it may begin to reflect the many hues of the Ineffable One, the heavenly Dragon Queen.

To clarify the mind so that we may reflect the eternal flame of the Divine, we need to meditate regularly. Five minutes each day makes a good beginning, although, as you come to enjoy meditation more and more, you will probably wish to extend this period to twenty minutes. If five minutes a day is too much for you at first, simply start with two. The important thing is that you do it.

Rose Meditation

We take for our first meditation symbol the beautiful form of a rose. It is our Dragon Chalice, from whose depths we absorb our sacred and divine Dragon heritage. The rose is pink, because it harmonizes the red and the white life forces, and we see it blooming in the heart centre. Gently stabilize your inner focus upon the rose in the heart, and inhale its pure fragrance.

Assume a rhythm whereby you breathe in the perfume of the rose, all the while keeping your inner gaze upon it, and absorb the entirety of its healing, calming, inspiring essence. Then breathe it out to the world. Just spend five minutes doing this peaceful exercise, or longer if you wish to.

Eternal Flame Meditation

Our next symbol is the eternal flame. It is the power of our Dragon form. (It is only necessary to work with one image each day, changing it as you prefer.)

See a flame of liquid light curling into the heavens. This mirror-bright flame might be a candle-flame, like the shape of two hands joined in prayer; or it might rise from some mystical source in the interior of the earth, ascending like an angel of purest light. It might be a flame like the northern lights, dancing its spirit dance in a swirl of mystical colours. This flame, too, is in your heart; breathe in its light, flood your entire being with its brilliance, and then breathe it out to the earthly world, for its blessing and healing.

Sword Meditation

Our third image is a sword of hallowed light. It is our Dragon keenness of spirit. Its blade of glory points upward. We wield it in our hearts, and we can reach into that centre and take it, still pointing upward, in our hand. We dispel the shadows that press in upon us with this sword. It tames the dragon of the lower self. It fills us with courage. Fear in all its manifold forms is driven away. See its light shooting upward in a streak of spiritual purity and beauty. If we ever seek to use it selfishly or violently, we shatter the sword.

We can still use the breath in conjunction with the sword, for we breathe in its holiness, its surety, its protection, and then breathe out these peace-yielding gifts to the world.

Silence Meditation

Our final symbol is that of Silence. This is the Dragon-stone, the Stone of Ascension associated with the Emerald Tablet. We might find this concept too obscure to be able to cope with it in meditation purely as a state of being. If so, we can imagine it as a ring of immaculate light, as of the vestal light in the brilliant flash of diamonds. Go through that ring of light as if you are crossing the threshold into a gem of unimaginable radiance, as if you are stepping into the heart of a boundless star. Dwell in the light, and be aware of your breath and the pulse of your heart. This is the rhythm of Silence, this is the pulse of Silence. Dwell in the hallows of the Silence, and send forth its pulsation of creative love into the human world that struggles below the heavens.

We will note that four symbols are given. They are the four symbols of the Grail, our Dragon heritage. They will help us in our bid to reclaim it. If you experience difficulty in accepting the idea that the symbols exist in the heart, just see the image as if face to face with it, with an inner knowing that its dwelling-place is the beautiful shrine in the heart centre.

When we sit for meditation, we ensure that we are comfortable and relaxed, and that our spine is as straight as possible (support it if this gives greater ease). When we emerge from meditation, we have to be careful to seal our higher centres (as is the case when 'touching down' after performing the angel ceremonies given in this book), for our own protection. This just takes a few seconds. In imagination, hold the symbol of a bright silver cross of light enclosed within a circle of light over the two crown centres, the brow centre, the throat centre, the heart centre, and over the solar plexus.

The symbol of the cross of light within the circle of light is the great Sign of the Dragon Queen, who bequeathed its protective force to Enki and his consort. It is the Mark of Cain, or kingship ('Cain' or 'Qayin' translates as 'king' or 'queen'). It is the symbol of the royal or exalted Dragon, the symbol of our highest humanity. We can use this great and glorious symbol as a mighty form of protection.

Practise creating it in an instantaneous sweep of the imagination. Stand within the intersection of the cross, at its heart, where a star of the fire of God burns with a measureless light. No darkness, no evil, can withstand this light. It must halt, turn back, hide its face. Assume your Dragon heritage, merge with the light of the star, and know that nothing can touch you. You are a being of perfect light. You are a child of God. You cannot be harmed or overcome. Nothing evil can come near you. All is well.

The beautiful six-pointed star, which is the source and the power of our heart-light, is the supreme key to the reclamation of our Dragonhood. It is formed from two equilateral triangles, one with its pinnacle pointing upward, and the other with its pinnacle pointing downward. The merging of these two triangles creates the six-pointed star but, unlike the Star of David, it bears no inner divisions. The fusion of the two triangles creates a flawless unity. It is expressed in a great blaze of supernal light.

The star is within our hearts. We find it by focusing gently on the breath, and letting its light shine forth. The star in our hearts connects with the great, blazing star in the heavens, the six-pointed star of the spiritual dimensions, for truly they are one. Having created the star, having summoned it into being, we know that the star is in our hearts, that we stand within the heart of the star, and that it also shines above us in the overarching skies of the spirit. These realities exist simultaneously.

Now we can project the light of the star. We do it with the out-breath, with the gentle, steady focus of the mind, with a blaze of love from the heart centre. If we find it difficult to feel love on command, then the trick is to *act* as if we are feeling that current of love. When we act with true intent rather than in order to deceive, the act itself forms a channel through which higher beings can nourish us with the genuine essence of what we are expressing. This is the crucial difference between dramatic art and sham, and the secret as to why great actors can move us so deeply. We act within ourselves, within our hearts, as if we conjured the outflow of love with a magical command. We know that it is there, we have faith that it goes forth from us – and it does.

There are special hours at which we can make a supreme connection with the star. They occur at the points of 3, 6, 9 and 12 o'clock throughout the 24-hour cycle. Twelve noon, the meridian, is the most powerful of all, being the heart centre of the day. If, whenever we can, we take a two-minute or even a one-minute break from whatever we are doing, and send forth this light with a spoken blessing on humanity and the world so that it encircles the planet, we will prepare ourselves and the Earth for the coming of the Grail.

We can project this light into our homes, our places of work, to local and international trouble spots, to people who are in need of help. The light may be radiated to animals, to places in nature, to gardens, even to individual trees and plants.

It is never forced on anyone, nor is it projected to bring into being any personal preference concerning another person's behaviour or decision. It is simply a free gift from the heart, for the recipient to accept or refuse as they will. Our dragon nature, our higher self, scintillates far above the pushiness and desire for control which belong to the ego, and brings that ego, the little earthly self, safely into the heart of the greater self, so that its humanity and its connectedness with earth remain, but its inharmonious aspects do not. They are caught up, transformed into a perfect energy, pulsating in rhythm with the divine light of the star – the light of God.

As we use the star, we will receive absolute confirmation of its truth and reality, and of the actuality of the spirit and the higher worlds from which it shines. We will no longer be tempted to think that the dull veil of the earth dimension is all that exists, or that we are helpless, impotent creatures living finite lives on an insentient ball of rock. We are dragons, and the worlds which are our birthright are glorious and infinite.

A number of people have been working with the star for several decades now (and many long before that, because the star is an ancient and eternal symbol). Not all such people may think of themselves as dragons – but in ethereal vision their astral forms are revealed as replete with many-coloured flourishing dragon crests and streaming manes of unfathomable light, with swirling tails or wings like outspread tongues of flame dancing through their auras. Truly we are dragons, and our Dragonhood is waiting for us to consciously assume it once again.

And now, the *amesha spentas*, the six great archangels representing the six-pointed star that came to Zarathustra and inspired his mighty mission, come to us again to enfold and overlight us. Around them and within them circulate the power and grace of Michael and Shekinah. They are with all humanity, calling to those who will listen and respond at this crucial and inspiring time. They are the great lords of the Ka angels, directing them to offer their kick-ass energies to us because they know, they see, that the seventh point of the ineffable star of light, that seventh point which is its completion, integrity and perfection, is humanity itself – humanity linked to the Light, the Son–Daughter, the Divine Child of God.

The mystery of God generates the Light, and is the Light. In the centre of the star stand Enki and his bride, urging us to accept the Light, our eternal inheritance, so that we may step into our fully human selves and become Pendragons, beings of unutterable light: the unconquered sun.